THE SUNDAY TIMES
PERSONAL FINANCE GUIDE RETIREMENT

DIANA WRIGHT

HarperCollins*Publishers*

HarperCollins Publishers
77-85 Fulham Palace Road
Hammersmith
London W6 8JB

The HarperCollins website address is www.**fire**and**water**.com

First published in 1996 by HarperCollins Publishers
This new, expanded edition published 2002

Copyright © Diana Wright 1996, 2002

ISBN 0 00 712191-1

The Sunday Times is a registered trademark of Times Newspapers Ltd

All rights reserved. No part of this publication may be reproduced, stored in a retrieval system or transmitted, in any form or by any means electronic, mechanical, photocopying, recording or otherwise without the prior written permission of the publisher and copyright holders.

British Library Cataloguing in Publication Data
A catalogue record for this book is available from the British Library.

Page design, typesetting and artwork by
Morgan Studios, Linlithgow EH49 6AQ

Printed and bound in Great Britain by
Omnia Books Ltd, Glasgow G64 2QR

Contents

Introduction		**1**
1	Planning your retirement – the groundwork	5
2	Pensions from the state	13
3	Company pensions	25
4	Saving extra for your pension	43
5	Individual pensions	53
6	The annuity choice	61
7	Insurance after retirement	75
8	Investing in retirement – finding advice	87
9	Planning your post-retirement portfolio	95
10	Low-risk investments	101
11	Medium-risk investments	111
12	Higher-risk investments	119
13	Investment planning in practice	131
14	Planning for the fourth age	147
15	Making a will	155
16	Inheritance tax planning	161
17	Planning for income and capital gains tax	167
Useful names, addresses and websites		**177**
Index		**185**

About the author

DIANA WRIGHT has been writing on personal finance issues since 1982. She edited *The Sunday Times Money* section for ten years to 1995 and since then has been a regular contributor to the paper. She is the editor of *The Sunday Times Guide to Personal Finance* and has written a number of other books. She has won numerous awards for writing on pensions, unit trusts and insurance, including the Association of British Insurers Lifetime Award for insurance journalism in 1998.

Introduction

This book will not tell you how to have a happy retirement, but it will help to ensure that it is, as far as possible, a financially comfortable one.

Most people do not want to spend long hours contemplating money problems – or even money solutions. After all, there are plenty of other interesting things to think about. But when we retire, our lives change dramatically. Part of this change will be financial, so it is essential to make plans for the future. A burst of activity now should stand you in good stead later. This guide aims to help you get your affairs on to a sound footing for your retirement, so that you will not be forced to spend too much precious time in the future thinking, or worrying, about your finances.

That said, some people enjoy managing their investments. As with so many other things in life, the more you know, the more interesting it becomes. But to do so successfully, you need to do a certain amount of groundwork and, hopefully, this book should help. If you are not particularly interested in money and investment, this book should be even more useful – if you act on it now, you can throw it away later!

For some people, understandably, retirement can appear to create more anxieties than enticing opportunities. Those retiring with membership of a good company pension scheme may have access to a significant lump sum, probably the largest they have ever had to deal with. The instinct is to put it somewhere "safe" (usually a building society account) because they cannot afford to lose it. This might be the best thing to do, but it should not be a decision that is taken automatically. Depending on your circumstances, there may well be a more rewarding – even a more prudent – solution.

The decisions taken at this stage in your life can be intimidating. When you are working, you can always use next month's pay cheque to help you out of temporary difficulties, or save hard for the next year or two to rebuild your nest egg after a financial setback. But when you are retired, this is no longer possible.

Within the vast financial services industry there are large numbers of people with considerable experience, knowledge and judgment. They are there to help you, but many of our readers' letters show that people are unwilling to put their trust wholeheartedly in someone they have not met before, particularly on such an important issue. They are not confident that they would be able to distinguish between good advice and bad.

Some parts of the industry have attracted – and deserved – bad publicity in recent years. Advice given has sometimes proved to be more in the interest of the salesperson or the adviser than the client. But don't be put off taking any advice because of this. There is a way round the problem, and that is to make sure you do sufficient groundwork yourself so that you know, broadly, what it is you are seeking and can recognise sensible advice.

Chapter 13 contains examples of investment problems and how they might be approached. The time difference between writing and publishing means that some factors, such as interest rates, may have changed, but the process is generally slower than we might imagine: the inflation rate may rise or fall month by month, but it's unlikely to double or halve over a few months; interest rates may be cut or hiked half a percentage point or more, but the broad relationship been inflation, interest rates and other potential returns tends to remain steady for many years at a time.

However, you should bear in mind that these examples are just that – examples – not recommendations on specific courses of action. They should give you an idea of how problems can be tackled and provide a rough benchmark against which you can judge whatever up-to-date, specific advice you may be given.

Planning of any sort means trying to predict the future and adjusting present-day actions in the light of those plans. Retirement planning involves (no use beating about the bush!) making a guess at how long you might live.

Life expectancy tables make unexpectedly cheery reading: the older you are, the longer still you are likely to be around. These tables, worked out by life insurance companies for their own ends, don't run out until the age of 112, at which point women have an average expectation of living another 1.05 years (though males peter out at the age of 109).

Table 1 shows average life expectancies from age 55 – the point at which an increasing number of people start thinking about early retirement. If you are trying to work out how to stretch your money over the rest of your life, you must conclude from this table that, unlike

Introduction

Charles II who supposedly apologised to the people gathered round his deathbed for taking "an unconscionable time dying", we spend an unconscionable time living.

Table 1
Life expectancy based on 1992 mortality tables

Age now	Average future life expectancy (years)	
	Men	Women
55	21.856	26.357
60	17.850	22.079
65	14.267	18.111
70	11.187	14.487
75	8.572	11.284
80	6.438	8.413
85	4.762	6.111
90	3.508	4.354

Source: Swiss Re Life and Health, UK

Although this table reflects the latest "official" figures, it is probably already behind the times. Something strange is happening: although we have all got used to the fact that things are, in general, getting better and people are living longer, there is, it seems, a "golden generation" – people born between 1925 and 1945 – for whom the improvement in mortality has jumped out of all proportion to those older or younger. Table 2 is an estimate from the same company, Swiss Re, of what the real situation is likely to be for people who are currently aged 55 and upwards. It can only be a guess – we won't know for certain until all today's 55-year-olds have died off and we can correlate the statistics – but it's as accurate as any guess can be.

Table 2
Life expectancy based on latest research

Age now	Average future life expectancy (years)	
	Men	Women
55	29.042	32.524
60	24.065	27.399
65	19.396	22.455
70	15.185	17.833
75	11.539	13.678
80	8.526	10.122
85	6.151	7.244
90	4.362	5.047

Source: Swiss Re Life and Health, UK

Of course, this improvement is great news, but it is also tough from a financial point of view. Your money in retirement is going to have to work hard to ensure it is still supporting you so far into the future.

If you are a long-term member of a good company pension scheme, then much – though not necessarily all – of that burden will be off your hands. But whatever your circumstances, some careful planning at this stage should improve your long-term prospects. I hope this book will help you to do just that.

1

Planning your retirement – the groundwork

Some people can hardly wait for retirement, while others avoid even thinking about it until the day arrives. But if you are willing to spend some time planning now, you should be able to make it a far more enjoyable experience. To help you, this chapter looks at:

◆ Planning a five-year approach to retirement
◆ Budgeting for life after work
◆ Saving money on current accounts, credit cards and insurance
◆ Mortgage tactics
◆ Reassessing your investment portfolio

If you're self-employed, you can just carry on working, putting off the evil day more or less indefinitely – although your partner might not be so happy with that arrangement. Even the most well-balanced individual is likely to approach retirement with feelings of both joy and trepidation – it is, after all, a landmark which may represent the biggest change to our lives since we left school or started our first job. Being a "learner" again after 30 or 40 years may be exciting but it is also an unsettling experience.

Major financial changes after retirement are often uppermost in people's minds, and if you think about and plan your finances you may well find yourself considering your broader situation in retirement. Ideally, you should start some serious planning a few years before the big day. If you are fortunate, you can construct your own timetable, although in recent years many people have had early retirement thrust on them as companies have cut their costs by cutting staff.

Timetable for your retirement

Everyone will have their own thoughts on this, but here are some ideas on how you can prepare for the big day.

Five years to go

- ◆ Consider whether you want to make any major structural alterations to your home. If so, embark on them now – get the mess out of the way before you're at home all day.
- ◆ Carry out a first check on the amount of pension you are likely to receive. Start additional savings if necessary.
- ◆ Will your mortgage be fully paid off by the time you retire? If not, consider making extra payments from now on to ensure that it is.

Four years to go

- ◆ Monitor your credit and store card spending. Running up debts on credit cards is a luxury for busy people with more money than sense (or time). If you habitually carry forward a large balance on your cards, start clearing it to ensure you are debt-free by retirement day. Do the same with any personal loans or overdrafts.

Three years to go

- ◆ Feeling the first inkling of the potential of life after work? Time to stock up on the kit for those hobbies you will soon be able to pursue. Buy the camera (or whatever) you have always promised yourself.
- ◆ Get tough with offspring – get them to clear out "their" bedrooms and nab the space for your darkroom, study or general hobby room. It will probably take at least three years for them to obey your edict, so issue it at once. Threaten to burn cherished collections of Action Men and Barbie dolls and, as a last resort, carry this out.

Two years to go

- ◆ Carry out a stocktaking exercise. Major household repairs and refurbishments should be carried out now, paying particular attention to the effect these might have on running costs. So, for instance, it may be worth replacing the central heating boiler, improving the insulation or installing double glazing.

- Run an eye over the rest of your white and brown goods – the washing machine, fridge, freezer, television and so on – and consider replacing them if they are becoming long in the tooth.
- Check your pension situation again. Increase pension savings if appropriate and possible. Alternatively, use an individual savings account (Isa) to build up your tax-free investments.

One year to go

- Time to look at transport. Do you drive a company car? Start thinking how you will replace it. Even if you don't, consider whether you should swap your expensive-to-run status symbol for something more efficient. Think about downsizing to one car – and buy a couple of bicycles, for sheer enjoyment as well as convenience and economy.
- Consider your post-retirement tax position. Now that you have a fairly clear idea of how much your pension is going to be, consider juggling any other investments you might hold to make use of both personal allowances. If one partner has only a small income, he or she should be the one to hold the bulk of your combined interest-producing investments.
- Start making a monthly budget of the typical running costs of your life. If you are married, this needs to be a joint exercise. Your overall running expenses will inevitably change after retirement because the nature of your life will change – but at least it will provide you with a starting point.

Costs of life after retirement

No great financial acumen is needed to work out the principal changes in costs after retirement: up will go heating and lighting, possibly motoring expenses (if you had a company car before) and there may well be increased expenditure on leisure activities; down will go the cost of smart clothes and commuting. Some changes may be less obvious, such as:

Up

- Telephone bills, now you can no longer phone from work.
- Small treats – cream teas in the country or whatever, now you can indulge yourself every day, not just at weekends.
- Paper, pens, photocopying, postage – not, of course, that you made a habit of using the office mailbag for private post, but…

Happily, most of these expenses are relative molehills in a well-ordered budget. In any case, you might not have thought of some of the possible decreases in running costs, such as:

Down

- Premiums for home contents insurance, now that the house is occupied more of the day.
- Premiums on car insurance, often available for "safer" older drivers.
- Banking costs, as you have time to seek out the best deal.
- Even food – now that you have the time to cook real meals and time to "pick your own" – and maybe even "grow your own".

Obviously, it is impossible to generalise about the effect of retirement on household budgets because we are all so different. How much we spend, and on what, is as much a reflection of who we are as our overall means. You may, in any case, find it difficult to predict precisely how your spending patterns will change until you have adjusted to your new life. Many people who have gone through the process report that during their first year or so of retirement, spending seems to rise dramatically. Don't panic, because it rarely continues at this rate. I suspect that, during that first year of adjustment, people find that time hangs heavy on their hands and money is needed to fill the holes. As they adjust to a different pace of life and perhaps embark on voluntary work or social activities close to their home, such spending tends to fall away.

Budget planning points

Current accounts

Most people still use a branch-based current account – inertia is a powerful factor – but as you embark on retirement, it could be the time to get to grips with internet banking. Branch-based current accounts do, mostly, pay interest on credit balances, but with a typical rate of 0.1%, you practically need a microscope to spot the benefit.

The internet accounts are the ones with the funny names which are already beginning to sound a bit dated, such as Smile (part of the Cooperative Bank), Cahoot (an offshoot of Abbey National) and Intelligent Finance (Halifax). Their interest rates are by no means old-fashioned, however – at the time of writing, they were paying between

3% and 5% on credit balances. A useful website to consult is www.moneyfacts.co.uk which, among other things, lists the top-paying current accounts.

Some people have had problems setting up internet accounts, and despite undertakings by the banks that it should take no longer than ten days to transfer all the standing orders and direct debits from one current account to another, there have been instances of it taking a great deal longer. But now that you have time on your hands – in theory, at least – it could be worth taking the plunge.

Credit and store cards

This is also a good time to count up just how many credit or store cards you have accumulated. One is quite enough for most people – and it may be possible to get one without an annual fee (with a second card on the same account thrown in). Some of the "free" card issuers turn down a lot of applicants: don't interpret this as a slur on your credit-worthiness – it may well be the reverse, as those who pay off their balance in full each month are the least attractive customers from the issuer's point of view. Secure a cheaper new card before getting rid of all your old ones.

Store cards, with the exception of the John Lewis card, tend to charge even higher rates of interest than credit cards, so if you do want to keep them, make sure they are used purely as a means of payment and not as a vehicle for credit. Finally on the plastic front, the charge cards, such as those issued by American Express and Diners Club, usually have the highest annual fees and this may be the time to let them go.

Insurance

Insurance companies have begun to realise that older people are better customers because they tend to make fewer claims ("older" generally means over 55) so if you have not done so already, look at your general insurance arrangements. Some leg-work in this area could lead to cuts in premiums of at least 5% to 10%.

As for home contents and car insurance, older people are quite simply a better bet. They are safer and steadier drivers, more honest in making claims and, when they are not clocking up their limited mileage driving sedately down the high street, they sit at home, deterring opportunistic burglars by their presence. All these factors cut the risk of big claims on such policies quite significantly – so premiums should be lower. And however remote this identikit picture might be from you as an individual, the fact you have reached that certain age should allow you to qualify for these reductions, assuming you have a reasonable claims record.

Premiums for buildings insurance are not affected by the age of the policyholder, but there may still be savings to be made, especially if you have stayed with the policy sold to you by your mortgage lender many years ago.

So how do you go about finding cheaper insurance? You can shop around either by telephone or on the internet, or use a broker or other intermediary. Some brokers specialise in the retired market: Age Concern, for example, has an insurance services division and there are a number of other specialist brokers. Contact details are in the names and addresses section at the end of the book.

If you prefer to shop around yourself, a good website to consult is www.find.co.uk which will link you to sites providing comparative quotations. If you don't have access to the internet, even a brief trawl of the market, by calling a few of the direct insurers plus consulting at least one broker, may well yield savings. And don't forget to ask your existing insurer whether it has any special deals for retired people. Home contents policies are beginning to offer no-claims discounts to policyholders, but unlike motor insurance, these cannot be transferred to a new company.

Your mortgage

Many people will have finished paying off their mortgage well before they retire. If you have a repayment mortgage, and you are within a few years of the end, it is well worth making extra payments now.

This is not just for the sake of tidiness – to get clear of the loan by the time you retire – but also because it could mean significant savings. Many repayment mortgages are still organised on an annual interest basis. Under this system, the lender calculates your monthly payments at the start of every year, basing the total amount of interest due over the coming 12 months on the size of the debt at the start and taking no account of the capital that is paid back during this time.

With a typical 25-year mortgage, in the early years practically all your payments consist of interest, with little in the way of capital repayment. But towards the end of the term, the situation is reversed. Most of each monthly payment is going to repay capital. This means the annual system becomes progressively more inaccurate as the years go by: you are, in effect, paying a lot more interest than you should.

So paying the loan off early will save you money. If you cannot pay it all back in one go, but want to make extra repayments, speak to your lender to find out when the extra payments will be credited. It is usually best to time them for just before the start of the lender's new financial year to make sure there is no time lag before they are credited.

Endowment mortgages

There has been plenty of bad press in recent years about endowment mortgages failing to meet their target. Nevertheless, if your endowment policy has been running for 20 or more years, it is likely to do so, even with something to spare.

Those with policies set up more recently may not be so fortunate, however. If you are in this position, you will probably have received a letter from your life company warning that the policy may not reach its target and suggesting that you pay extra premiums to keep it on track.

In fact, you have several options, but what you must not do is simply ignore the problem. First, consider whether you have grounds for a complaint that the policy was mis-sold. The Financial Services Authority has a free factsheet entitled *Endowment Mortgage Complaints* (to order, call 0845 606 1234) setting out what you should have been told at the time the policy was sold. For instance, it should have been made clear that an endowment is a long-term commitment that often gives a poor return if cashed in early and that it does not guarantee to pay off the loan. In some cases, the fact that the endowment was set up to last beyond normal state retirement age has also been grounds for a successful complaint.

If the complaint is upheld, you may be eligible for compensation, but only if you have lost out financially as a result of the bad advice.

If you have no grounds for complaint, you may still have the problem of how to meet the possible shortfall. Increasing the endowment premiums is one solution, or you could consider setting up a separate savings plan, perhaps linked to an individual savings account (Isa). But the simplest and safest way is to make extra repayments from now on. Contact your lender and get it to work out appropriate figures for you.

Planning your retirement portfolio

Your investment needs may well change as you enter retirement, with a greater emphasis on income-producing investments and security. But you should resist the temptation – either before or after retirement – to embark on a wholesale rearrangement of your portfolio in one fell swoop. There are two good reasons: first, capital gains tax, payable on any gains above the annual exempt limit (£7,500 in the 2001-02 tax year) and, second, the danger of getting the timing wrong. It is only with hindsight that it is easy to tell the right time to sell investments; some people manage it, but most don't. Spreading out sales and purchases over a few years will help in both respects. It should cut down the CGT bill, while ensuring, at the least, that you won't be selling all your investments at the worst possible time.

2
Pensions from the state

Planning your retirement finances has to start with pensions, and for many people that will mean at least two sources of income: pensions from the state and a pension from one or more previous employers. This chapter looks at the various state pension schemes, along with the main types of state help for those on lower incomes, including:

◆ When you can get a state pension
◆ How much you can expect
◆ How to get it
◆ Extra help for poorer pensioners
◆ The new pension credit
◆ Other payments to pensioners
◆ Where to get more information

Successive governments have jigged and rejigged pensions benefits and the process continues. Anyone coming up to retirement today may be entitled to three different types of government pension:
◆ The basic state pension
◆ Graduated retirement benefit
◆ The state earnings-related pension scheme (Serps)

State retirement age

Pensions are payable weekly from age 65 for men and, currently, from age 60 for women. But the retirement age for women is set to rise, in stages, with the eventual result that women, like men, will become eligible only at age 65.

Any woman born before 6 April, 1950 will qualify for her pension at 60. Women born on or after 6 April, 1955 will get it at 65. If you were born between these dates, there is a sliding scale and the date you qualify for the pension depends on the month and year in which you were born. Table 3 gives examples of how the age rises. You can find a full table showing pension dates for all ages in the booklet NP46: *A Guide to Retirement Pensions*, which is available from social security offices. This extensive booklet (100 pages in its latest edition) is really the "bible" for all matters relating to state pensions.

Table 3
How state retirement age rises for women born after 6 April, 1950

Date of birth	Pensionable age (in years/months)	Pension date
06/04/1950 – 05/05/1950	60/00 – 60/01	6/05/2010
06/01/1951 – 05/02/1951	60/09 – 60/10	6/11/2011
06/03/1952 – 05/04/1952	61/11 – 62/00	6/03/2014
06/07/1953 – 05/08/1953	63/03 – 63/04	6/11/2016
06/05/1954 – 05/06/1954	64/01 – 64/02	6/07/2018
06/03/1955 – 05/04/1955	64/11 – 65/00	6/03/2020

The basic state pension

The basic state pension is payable to everyone who has paid or been credited with sufficient National Insurance contributions (NICs).

It is increased each April, usually in line with price inflation. In November 2001, the government announced that the increase would never be less than £100 a year. Occasionally it will award a higher increase. For the tax year April 2001-02, the full pension rates are:
- Single person: £3,770
- Dependant's addition: £2,256.80
- Total married pension: £6,026.80

There is also a tax-free Christmas bonus of £10 and pensioners over the age of 80 get an extra 25p a week.

The basic state pension may sound like small beer to anyone who is well off, but to put it into context, a man would have to have a capital sum of well over £100,000 to provide an income equivalent to the married couple's full pension of £6,026 a year. And a woman would need a good £80,000 to give her a guaranteed index-linked income equivalent to the pension of £3,770 from age 60.

Who gets the basic pension?

To qualify you must have paid some NICs – either a full year's worth (April to April) after 1975 or a total of 50 weekly contributions before then. Anyone who has paid or been credited with sufficient NICs of the right sort – roughly 90% of the theoretical maximum – is entitled to the full basic pension. Those who have paid less get less. In some circumstances, it is possible to make up the difference by paying extra NICs before retirement.

The basic pension and married women

If you have worked only a little, or not at all, and do not qualify for a pension in your own right, you can get one based on your husband's contributions provided he is over 65 and has claimed his own retirement pension. If he qualifies for the maximum, he would receive the single person's pension of £3,770 and you would receive the maximum dependant's addition of £2,256.80, which together make up the total married pension of £6,026.80.

If you qualify in your own right for some basic pension, but for less than the full amount of the dependant's addition, it can be topped up to this level. But if your own basic pension is higher, you will not get any more based on your husband's contributions. This calculation is carried out automatically.

How to claim

The Department of Work and Pensions should send you a claim form, number BR1, a few months before you reach your state retirement age. If you do not receive the form within, say, three months of your relevant birthday, you should contact it.

How the basic pension system works

The system works by establishing the number of years of your "working life" – currently 49 for a man and 44 for a woman. The amount of pension you get then depends on the number of "qualifying" years – those for which you have been paid or credited with the appropriate class of NICs. A record of about 90% will mean you qualify for the full pension; any less, and you get less, on a sliding scale.

Table 4 gives a summary of what you'll get if you have paid less. For fuller details, see booklet NP46.

Table 4
How much of the basic pension will you qualify for?

Women Number of qualifying years	% of pension	Men Number of qualifying years	% of pension
0-9	Nil	0-10	Nil
10	26%	11	25%
15	39%	15	35%
20	52%	20	46%
25	65%	25	57%
30	77%	30	69%
35	90%	35	80%
39 or more	100%	40	91%
		44 or more	100%

Note: the figures for women are for those born on or before 5 October, 1950. Women born after that will for qualify for lower percentages depending on their year of birth. Those born on or after 6 October, 1954 will need the same qualifying years as men.

This table assumes that the working life starts at age 16 and runs until age 60 or 65. But there are some circumstances that allow you to be credited for years you did not work.

Education

Children who stay on full-time at school until age 18 will be credited as if they had paid the appropriate NICs, so these will count as qualifying years. Students at university or in other forms of higher education are not credited in this way. They can catch up later by paying voluntary class 3 NICs, but there is a time limit of six years after the end of their course.

Bringing up children or looking after the sick

People who take time off work to bring up children or to look after someone who is sick or disabled can receive "home responsibilities protection" (HRP). This means they need fewer qualifying years to build up an entitlement to a pension: a minimum of 20 qualifying years for a full pension, while a lower number will provide a reduced pension.

You do not actually have to have stayed at home during your HRP years – you might have worked on a temporary basis from time to time, without staying long enough to build up a record of qualifying years by paying NICs throughout a tax year.

You should have been given HRP automatically for any full tax year in which you got child benefit, or income support for looking after someone sick or disabled. But it has to be you, not your partner, who received the child benefit. In other circumstances, you might have to apply for HRP. To do so, you would need form CF411, available from social security offices.

Note that HRP is not awarded for any tax year before 1978–79.

Getting a pension forecast

This is only a summary of a labyrinthine system. But while it is useful to understand the basics, the government will do the specific calculations for you. The best thing to do is to get a pension forecast a few years before retirement. This will be useful not just for your general planning, but also because you might be able to make extra NI contributions now to increase your entitlement. There is a time limit in respect of missed contributions of six years, so even if you are still a few years away from retirement, it may be worth doing sooner rather than later.

To obtain a pension forecast, complete form BR19, available from social security offices or from 0191 218 7585 or apply online at www.dwp.gov.uk.

The forecast is based on your current contribution record. It can be requested any time up to four months before state retirement age.

If your record is patchy, your local office can tell you if it is possible for you to make voluntary contributions now – bearing in mind the six-year rule – and if so, how much is required. For more information on this get leaflets CA08: *National Insurance: Voluntary Contributions* and CA07: *National Insurance – Unpaid and Late Paid Contributions* from your local office.

Continuing to work after state retirement age

If you do not give up work at the minimum state retirement age, the good news is that you do not have to pay any more NI contributions. You should automatically get a certificate of age exemption (form CF384) when you claim your pension, which you should then hand to your employer – if you decide to defer claiming your pension, you can ask your social security office for one. Your employer, however, does have to carry on paying its NI contributions on your behalf.

If you are self-employed, you do not have to pay any more class 2 contributions (the flat-rate ones) and you stop paying class 4 contributions from the start of the tax year after the one during which you reached state retirement age.

If you want, you can postpone taking your state pension for up to five years, in which case it will be increased. See the section "Postponing your state pensions" on page 20.

Retiring before state pension age

If you retire before the age of 60, you should consult your social security office; you may be advised to pay voluntary NI contributions (class 3) to protect your pension entitlement. However, men who retire after they have reached 60 but before 65 will normally have contributions automatically credited. From April 2010 (when the state retirement age for women will be 65) this will apply to both sexes.

Basic pensions for people over 80

If you are not entitled to any other state pension, from the age of 80 you will receive one anyway, as long as you are living in the UK on your 80th birthday and have been here for ten years or more since your 60th birthday. The current rate for this pension is £43.40 a week. If you do have a state pension but for less, it will be topped up to this level.

Graduated retirement benefit

This was a state scheme that ran from 1961 to 1975. Anyone who paid graduated NI contributions during this period may get a pension based on these, but the overall amounts will be small: the most you can receive is £7.70 a week for a man and £6.45 for a woman. Once payments have started, they will be increased each year in line with inflation. Any amounts due under this scheme will be included in the pensions forecast provided by your social security office.

State earnings-related pension scheme (Serps)

Serps arrived in April 1978 and is still with us, although many people are automatically "contracted out" through their membership of a company pension scheme and others have been encouraged to contract out by changes implemented by the government since the late 1980s. The self-employed are also largely excluded. Serps is being replaced in 2002 by a new state second pension, called S2P, but the amount already built up will be safeguarded.

Who gets it?

Employees who have paid the full standard rate class 1 NICs on a specific band of earnings for the whole of any tax year since April 1978 will have some Serps entitlement. You can qualify for some Serps pension (and some graduated retirement benefit) even if you have not built up sufficient years of contributions to get a basic state pension.

How much do you get?

Serps is designed as a top-up to the basic pension. It relates to a specific band of earnings, between a lower and an upper level. These are increased each tax year: for the 2001-02 tax year, they are £72 a week for the lower and £575 for the upper level. Any amounts you earn above the upper level are wasted as far as Serps is concerned.

The amount you get will depend on your total earnings between the two levels for each tax year since 1978. The original aim of Serps was to provide a maximum pension of 25% of the average "band earnings" you had received (revalued in line with wage inflation) after being a member of Serps for the full 20 years. But the entitlement was progressively cut for people retiring after April 2000 with the aim that, by 2010, those retiring then would get a Serps pension equivalent to only 20% of their band earnings covering the period from 1988-89 onwards.

But this change has itself been superseded, although it has scarcely started to bite, and a new scheme, known as the state second pension, starts in April 2002. The basics of this will be similar, in that it will use the concept of earnings between a lower and upper limit, but it will provide considerably higher pension sums to the low paid, to carers and to people with a long-term illness or disability.

Trying to work out your Serps entitlement would be a seriously tedious task, though if you are determined, booklet NP46 includes a worked example. You can, however, get a pension forecast by filling in form BR19 (see page 17) which automatically includes Serps and graduated pension entitlements along with the basic state pension.

Serps pensions, like the other state pensions, are increased in line with price inflation once they start being paid.

Widows and widowers

There are now different sets of rules, depending on when you reach state retirement age:
- If your spouse reaches state retirement age before 6 October, 2002, you can inherit all their Serps pension after their death.
- If they are younger, the amount that can be inherited is less. If they do not reach state retirement age until 6 October, 2010 or later, the amount you will be able to inherit is limited to 50%.
- If they are due to reach state retirement age between these two dates, there is a sliding scale, progressively reducing the percentage from 100% to 50%.

Widowers can inherit their wives' Serps pension only if they were both over pension age when she died.

Postponing your state pensions

If you want, you can delay receiving your pension for up to five years after your state retirement age. You can even change your mind, starting to draw the pension and then postponing it – but you can do this only once. And a married man who wants to defer his pension has to get his wife's consent if hers is based on his contributions, because if he defers his, she will have to defer hers, too.

If you do decide to defer, your pension will increase by about 7.5% for each full year you delay, with pro-rata increases for shorter periods, but you need to delay it for at least seven weeks to gain any increase.

Is it worth deferring it? Probably not, even if you don't really need the money now. A bird in the hand is always better than one in the bush, and your heirs will receive no benefit if you delay taking it and then step under a bus. There might be a case for delaying it if you are still working and the pension could tip you over into a higher tax band, from 22% to 40%, say, or from 10% to 22%. One possibility would be to take the pension anyway and invest it in a stakeholder pension plan, which means you will automatically get tax relief on the contributions. The following example shows how this could work:

> Andrew Morris retired – as an employee – aged 65 and decided to start drawing his state pension immediately. However, he is continuing to work as a consultant for a client of his former employer and his income from this, together with a comfortable company pension, means his marginal rate of income tax is still 40%.
>
> As he is still earning, he is entitled to put all of his basic state pension – £3,770 a year – into a stakeholder pension, and because his contributions benefit from 40% tax relief, this means he can save a gross amount of £6,283 per year. After five years, he gives up work completely. Assuming his stakeholder pension fund grows at 5% a year, he will have £36,453 at the end of the five years, which will buy him (at current rates) an index-linked pension of £2,880. Added to his state pension, this means a total index-linked income of £6,650, whereas if he had delayed taking the state pension, it would have grown by 7.5% for each year of delay, so (ignoring cost of living increases) it would be worth £5,184 after five years.
>
> Overall, then, it is worthwhile for Morris to take his state pension and invest it in a stakeholder plan for the five years that he carries on working. Getting the 40% tax relief on his contributions makes all the difference; if he had qualified for only basic rate relief at 22%, this course of action would still work in his favour, but the figures would be marginal – his total index-linked pension (stakeholder plus state) would amount to £5,985 compared to £5,184. Also, these figures assume that the pension fund will grow by 5% a year and that annuity rates remain stable. This is by no means guaranteed – there is a risk involved, whereas the increase in the state pension is guaranteed.

From 2010, 65-year-olds will be able to defer taking their state pension indefinitely and the rate of increase for each year of deferral will be 10.4% rather than the 7.5% today.

State pensions and income tax

Tax is never deducted from state pensions. This does not, of course, mean that they are tax-free, although if the basic pension is your sole income, it will be covered by your annual tax-free personal allowance. However, where a wife is more than five years younger than her husband, the dependant's addition of £2,256.80 counts as the husband's income (and is, therefore, taxable as his) until she reaches 60. Once she passes that age, it is treated as her income and can be set against her tax-free allowance.

Extra help for poorer pensioners

The basic state pension is still the largest source of income for most people over retirement age – and given that the single pension amounts to less than 18% of national average earnings these days, you can see just how little most pensioners have to live on.

There is extra government help available, principally in the form of income support for the very poorest pensioners. The concept of the minimum income guarantee (MIG) was introduced a couple of years ago and guarantees that pensioners will have a minimum income level (including the pension) which rises each year. The figures for the 2001-02 tax year are: £92.15 a week for a single person and £140.55 for a married couple. The intention is that the MIG will be increased each year in line with average earnings, rather than price inflation.

The MIG is means-tested; anyone with savings of more than £12,000 (£16,000 if they are living full-time in residential care or a nursing home) does not qualify at all, and those with savings of £6,000 plus (£10,000 for those in care) will get a reduced amount.

The pension credit

The problem with the MIG from the government's point of view is that it discourages saving. There's little point accumulating money to provide extra income in retirement if all it does is bring your total income up to the level of the MIG. So from the tax year starting in April 2003, a pension credit is proposed allowing people with modest savings or a small non-state pension to benefit from a higher MIG than those without.

In the tax year starting in April 2003, it is proposed that the basic MIG will be £100 for single pensioners and £154 for married couples. For every £1 of extra income above the state pension, pensioners' MIG will be increased by 60p, up to a maximum income of £135 (single people) and £201 (couples).

Other help for pensioners

There are two other government handouts for older people, neither of which is means-tested.
- **Winter fuel payments** These are payable to anyone living in the UK who is over 60. The current payment is £200 per eligible household, and it will continue at this level for the remainder of this parliament. To qualify for the winter of 2001-02, people had to be aged 60 or over during the week of 17-23 September.
- **TV licences** These are free for households which include someone aged over 75.

More information on state pensions and benefits

There are plenty of booklets and leaflets available to help you through the maze of state pensions. They should be available in social security offices, public libraries and post offices. You can also find them on the internet. The main sites are:
- www.inlandrevenue.gov.uk which publishes leaflets on National Insurance contributions.
- www.dss.gov.uk which publishes some of the leaflets and booklets on pensions and social security benefits.
- www.dwp.gov.uk which also publishes leaflets and booklets on pensions.

Voluntary organisations which can help with this highly complex area include:
- **The Citizens' Advice Bureau** Your local office will be in the phone book or see www.adviceguide.org.uk.
- **Age Concern** This has a network of branches. Its website is www.ageconcern.org.uk and the central telephone number is 0800 009966.
- **Help the Aged** This operates a telephone advice service, Seniorline, on 0808 800 6565. Its website is www.helptheaged.org.uk and the email address for enquiries is info@helptheaged.org.uk.

The voluntary organisations can be especially useful in helping you get an overall picture of your pension and benefits situation.

3
Company pensions

About ten million workers in this country are entitled to a company pension of one sort or another. If you're one of them, as you approach retirement, you may well want answers to the following questions:

- How much will my pension be?
- How much can I take as a tax-free cash sum?
- If I take it, how much will my pension be?
- How would early retirement affect my pension?
- How can I trace pensions from companies I used to work for?
- Where do I go if I have a problem with my company scheme?
- What are the tax rules on contributions and benefits?

How much will my pension be?

Until you have a reasonably accurate answer to this question, you cannot embark on any other financial planning. A few people will be able to find the answer without much difficulty.

If you have worked for the same company all your life and it has a good final salary scheme, you will probably get a pension of somewhere between one half and two-thirds of your final salary. Exactly how much and whether, for instance, the pension will increase in line with prices after retirement are matters that can usually be found out easily enough by reading your scheme's booklet or calling your company's pensions department.

But for most people, the answer is a lot less clear cut. There are two very different types of company pension scheme:
◆ Final salary (sometimes called defined benefit) schemes
◆ Money purchase (sometimes called defined contribution) schemes
It is quite possible that someone with a varied employment record will have accumulated pension rights under both types. However, because they work in different ways, they need to be dealt with separately.

Final salary schemes

These give employees a fraction of their final salary on retirement for each year they have worked for their company. Under Inland Revenue rules, the maximum pension you are allowed is generally two-thirds of final salary, and to get this you must have worked for that company for a minimum of either ten or 20 years, depending on when you joined the scheme – see the section on Inland Revenue rules on pages 39 to 41.

That is the absolute maximum that the Inland Revenue allows, but you would be pretty lucky to get it. Most good company schemes operate on a fraction of 1/60th of final salary for each year of service. This means that you will get a pension of two-thirds final salary only if you have worked for that company for 40 years.

The contributions an employee must make to a final salary scheme vary. A few companies ask for nothing at all, but between 4% and 8% of salary is more usual. The company pays the balance required.

You can decide to take part of your pension in the form of a tax-free cash sum, the maximum generally being one-and-a-half times salary after 20 years' service.

How much will I get?

Assuming you have worked for one company all your life and belonged to its pension scheme for the whole time, working out your pension is an easy matter. Once you've found out what fraction your scheme is based on, it is a matter of multiplying the number of years you will have worked by the time you retire by the fraction concerned, then multiplying the result by your current salary.

If you are certain of promotion between now and retirement, you could bump up your salary to what you expect to be earning in your final days. But if you are anticipating only normal pay rises, then my advice is to ignore them. Normal pay rises these days tend to be inflation plus a little bit more, but not much – and if you want to plan ahead properly, you need to know the real value of your likely pension, in terms of today's purchasing power. Here are a couple of examples:

Length of service:	37 years
Scheme based on:	1/60th of final salary for each year worked
Final salary:	£40,000
Retirement pension:	37 x 1/60th x £40,000 = £24,666.66
Length of service:	28 years
Scheme based on:	1/70th of final salary for each year worked
Final salary:	£25,000
Retirement pension:	28 x 1/70th x £25,000 = £10,000

Pension schemes for most civil servants and other employees in the public sector are set up rather differently. Typically, they provide a pension of 1/80th of final salary for each year worked – but they also provide a tax-free cash sum of up to one-and-a-half years' final salary in addition to their pension. Employees in the private sector can also get a cash sum, but this comes out of their pension entitlement, which will be lower as a consequence – see below.

You should note that what counts is usually the number of years you have been a member of the pension scheme, rather than the number of years you have worked for the company. In the past, it was not uncommon for companies to allow employees to join their pension scheme only once they had reached a certain age – maybe 25.

If you do not feel like doing the calculation yourself, you can ask your pensions department. You have a legal right to ask for a statement which includes details of your benefits both now and if you remain as a member until normal retirement age.

Taking tax-free cash

All company schemes allow you to take a tax-free cash sum on retirement which comes out of your pension entitlement. The theoretical maximum under Inland Revenue rules is one-and-a-half times final salary, available after 20 years' service (or two-and-a-quarter times your pension if this is greater, for people who joined their scheme after June 1989). In practice, most schemes provide the maximum only after 40 years' service. So someone with 40 years' service retiring on a final income of £40,000, say, would be allowed to take £60,000 in cash.

If you do take the cash, your pension will be reduced. But by how much? It depends on your scheme. If you want to know, roughly, in advance, you should ask your pensions department what "commutation factor" it uses. The answer could well be nine for someone retiring at 65 and 11 for someone retiring at 60.

What you do is divide the cash sum you can expect by nine (or 11) and the result is the amount of annual pension you will give up if you take it. Suppose, for instance, that you expect to be eligible for a cash sum of £50,000 at a retirement age of 65. If you divide £50,000 by nine the answer is £5,555. This means your pension will be reduced by £5,555 a year.

The higher the commutation factor, the less pension you will have to give up. There has been a tendency for factors to rise in recent years. That makes it sound as if company schemes are getting more generous, but the main reason behind this is that – thanks to falling interest rates and rising longevity – the cost of providing a pension has been rising sharply. So it saves the company money in the long run if you give up part of your pension for a cash sum.

Understandably, companies are not always willing to guarantee a commutation figure if you are asking them five or more years before your retirement, but most big schemes tend to stick with the same factor for years at a time, so whatever your scheme is currently using should be a good indication.

Taking early retirement

Retiring even a few years early can have a much bigger impact on your pension than you might imagine, because of the "double whammy" of fewer years' worth of contributions and investment growth, plus more years during which you will be drawing the pension. Some examples of the typical amount of pension you might lose are shown in table 5 on page 30. These could understate the true loss if, by leaving early, you miss out on a promotion that would have increased your salary by more than inflation.

If employers are so minded, there is often significant scope for them to improve the benefits of early retirees within the overall Inland

Revenue limits. A long-serving, valued worker who has to leave early because of ill-health, for instance, might be granted the full pension he or she would have received at normal retirement date (although this will be based on current earnings rather than some notional future figure).

More common – but still very generous – is the stance of companies who allow early retirees the full value of the pension rights they have accumulated so far. For example, a man who had worked for 20 years in a company with a 1/60ths pension scheme and who retired at 60 rather than the normal 65 could be given a pension of one third (20/60ths) of his final salary, payable from the date of his early retirement. Strictly speaking, he should get less, because his pension will be paid for an extra five years.

So what is strictly fair? Most companies operate a system whereby the pension is scaled down by a certain percentage for each year someone retires early. The typical percentage is 4%, though it may be slightly lower. Retiring five years early with a 4% reduction means, therefore, a reduction in pension of 20%. For example, a worker in the same circumstances as the man above, whose final salary was £30,000, would be entitled, before the scaling down, to a pension of £10,000 (one-third of final salary). Scaling down, this leaves him with just £8,000.

There may be some scope for negotiating with your employer if you want – or perhaps are being persuaded – to take early retirement. Big companies engaged in downsizing may be reasonably generous when encouraging employees to retire early. A company might, for example, credit you with not just your total years of service but also half the number of years between now and normal retirement.

If you think you have the negotiating clout, it is worth emphasising to your employer that its offer could almost certainly be enhanced while staying within the Inland Revenue maximum limits. For full details on these, see the section at the end of this chapter.

Table 5
The effect of early retirement on final salary pension schemes

These figures assume a final salary at retirement of £30,000 and a scheme which, at normal retirement date, gives members a pension of 1/60th of final salary for each year of service. The scaling down figure used is 4%.

	Retiring early		vs	Retiring at normal date	
No of years retiring early	No of years of service	Early retirement pension		Pension at normal date (after)	No of years of service
10	10	£3,000		£10,000	20
10	20	£6,000		£15,000	30
10	30	£9,000		£20,000	40
5	10	£4,000		£7,500	15
5	20	£8,000		£12,500	25
5	30	£12,000		£17,500	35
3	10	£4,400		£6,500	13
3	20	£8,800		£11,500	23
3	30	£13,200		£16,500	33
1	10	£4,800		£5,500	11
1	20	£9,600		£10,500	21
1	30	£14,400		£15,500	31

Money purchase schemes

This is the second type of company pension scheme, which is rapidly growing in popularity – with employers, at least, if not with employees. Many companies have decided to close their final salary schemes for new workers in favour of money purchase, while new company pension schemes are almost invariably set up on a money purchase basis. These are also known as defined contribution schemes, as opposed to the final salary-type of defined benefit schemes.

With a money purchase scheme, the employer and (usually) the employee both pay in a fixed contribution on a monthly or annual basis – perhaps 8% of salary from the employer plus another 4% from the employee – which is then invested in a managed pension fund. Each year, the company's pensions department has to provide members with a note of exactly how much their fund is worth. On retirement, it is used to buy a pension annuity.

The amount of the contributions varies widely, depending on the employer's generosity. Some lucky employees belong to schemes which are non-contributory – in other words, the employer makes a contribution but takes nothing from employees. Other schemes require a constant contribution from employees (say, 4% of salary) but have different rates of company contribution depending on their age – maybe 5% for the under 35s, 7% for those aged up to 50 and 10% for older workers.

Some schemes will have just one investment fund, into which all contributions are invested; others might offer employees a choice of two or three funds with different degrees of risk and potential reward.

How much will I get?

While you can find out easily enough how much money is going into your scheme each year and the current value of your own fund, you cannot know how much pension you are going to get at retirement. That depends on a number of factors:

◆ Investment growth rates between now and retirement.
◆ The amount of future contributions, including any additional ones made by employees under an additional voluntary contribution (AVC) scheme.
◆ Annuity rates which, in turn, depend on the general level of long-term interest rates and on average life expectancy at the time of your retirement. Annuity rates also depend on your age at retirement and your sex. Because women live longer than men and so draw their pensions for longer, annuity rates tend to be lower for them.

Table 6 gives some examples of annuity rates at various ages. These applied when bank base rate was 4.5% and the average yield on long-term gilts was around 4.7%. If long-term interest rates are a great deal higher when you retire, you will probably get better annuity rates than this, though it's not something you can count on. As people in general are living longer, the long-term trend has been for annuity rates to fall, as the annuity providers – the life companies – are having to pay out those annuities for longer.

People with a money purchase pension scheme are usually allowed to play the market and take their pension fund at retirement to the company providing the best annuity rates. Or their employer may well organise this on their behalf. They may be given a choice of the frequency with which payments are made – monthly, quarterly or annually, for example.

Table 6
The amount of annual pension you will get for a lump sum of £10,000

	Flat pension	Pension increasing at: 5% a year	RPI linked
Single man 60	£762	£448	£549
Single woman 60	£684	£371	£470
Single man 65	£862	£549	£650
Single woman 65	£754	£442	£542
Man 65 + wife 60 *	£724	£410	£511

Payments are monthly in advance and shown before tax
*Pension reduces to two-thirds on the first death

Source: Legal & General/Moneyfacts

Your future pension – how to guess

For all the reasons mentioned above, there is no way to know in advance what your pension will be under a money purchase scheme, but you can make a guess. Once you know the value of your pension fund, you can see from the annuity table above how much pension that sum would buy today. You can add to its current value the contributions you and your employer will be making between now and your retirement and work it out on that basis.

With luck, your fund will also benefit from growth in the underlying investments, but my advice would be to ignore that because it is not something you can count on – as we have all seen, stock markets can fall as well as rise and the value of pension funds along with them.

Investment considerations

Money purchase schemes pose some particularly tricky investment problems and anyone within a few years of retirement should devote some thought to them. The basic problem is that most of these funds are invested in shares – which offer the best prospects for long-term growth but can be volatile in the short term.

Once you are within a few years of retirement, your pension savings are no longer long term and you run the risk of years of planning and saving being blown off course by a collapse in the stock market just when you plan to retire.

Many company schemes recognise these risks and have special procedures for employees who are within, say, five years of retirement. They may offer you a lower-risk fund for your future contributions. They might also suggest that you switch across your existing fund, over a period of five years, so that once you are within a few months of retirement, all your pension savings are sheltered from the risks of a stock market crash and invested in gilts and other fixed-interest securities.

You will have to find out from your pensions department exactly what your scheme offers. Sometimes, a switch into lower-risk investments is made automatically once employees reach a certain age; sometimes, the choice is left up to the employee.

There is no right answer as to what you should do – except with hindsight. But for most people, it is probably sensible to err on the side of caution. It may mean you lose out on some growth by switching out of equities, but that is probably better than running the risk of seeing your pension fund collapse thanks to a drop in the stock markets just before you retire.

Taking tax-free cash

As mentioned above, all company pension schemes allow you to take a tax-free cash sum on retirement which comes out of your pension entitlement. The theoretical maximum under Inland Revenue rules is one-and-a-half times final salary, available after 20 years' service. In practice, most schemes provide this only after 40 years.

Taking the cash reduces your pension. With a money purchase scheme, the figures are relatively easy to work out. If you are entitled to, say, £10,000 cash and your total pension fund is £100,000, then your pension will be reduced by 10%.

Taking early retirement

Retiring early means less money going into your fund and a shorter time for it to benefit from investment growth. It also means your pension will be based on less favourable annuity rates, because it is going to be payable for longer. The following example shows how these factors combine to reduce the pension from what you might have expected had you stayed until the normal retirement date.

John Wilmot has built up a pension fund of £100,000 within his company's money purchase pension scheme when he decides to take early retirement at 60, five years before his company's normal retirement date. On a salary of £30,000 he could have expected total contributions into the fund of, say, 12% (£3,600) a year. By leaving five years early, he has lost contributions totalling at least £18,000 (disregarding any extra to reflect pay rises he might have had) and he has also lost out on extra years of investment growth.

Had Wilmot stayed on, assuming modest investment returns averaging 5% a year, his fund would have grown to about £145,600. As it is, he must make do with £100,000 which will buy him a pension of about £7,600. Because he is retiring younger, annuity rates are lower. If he stayed on until he was 65, his fund of £145,600 would probably buy him a pension of about £12,500.

The tax-free cash sum: should you take it?

Whether you have a final salary or money purchase scheme, you will be faced with the choice of whether to take the lump sum on retirement. Taking the cash, as we have seen, reduces your pension, so should you do it? Most people decide to, maybe using it for a special holiday to mark the start of a new phase of their life.

But perhaps you have done your sums and found that your retirement income is going to be fairly stretched. Should you forgo the lump sum and opt for the higher pension? There are reasons why you might still want to take the cash: it will be more flexible and you will be able to leave something to your heirs (whereas a pension dies with you or your widow or widower).

Even if income is your prime consideration, it might still be wise to take the cash and use it to buy an ordinary annuity. These work in the same way as pension annuities – they provide a regular income, guaranteed for life, in return for a lump sum – but they are taxed more lightly than pension annuities. The end result is that you might enjoy a higher income after tax by opting for the cash. Here's one example:

James Black, who is unmarried, retires at 65 after 40 years' service on a salary of £30,000, giving him a company pension of £20,000 a year. Alternatively, he can take a lump sum of £45,000 (one-and-a-half times final salary) and a reduced pension of £16,250 (his company uses a commutation factor of 12 – see page 28).

Investing the lump sum in an ordinary annuity provides Black with a gross income of £3,735. After tax, the annuity pays £3,501, while the net income from the top £3,750 of his full pension would amount to only £2,925.

In terms of immediate income, therefore, he is better off by more than £500 a year if he takes the cash and uses it to buy an ordinary annuity. However, he should remember that this annuity will not increase in line with inflation, unlike his company pension, which may do so.

Taking the lump sum to invest in an ordinary annuity will usually provide a better after-tax income but it is impossible to be certain, making this an area where independent advice can be very useful. The answer will depend on:

◆ **The rate obtained for the ordinary annuity** Rates differ from company to company – at the time of writing the best rate for a £10,000 level annuity for a single man of 65 was £844 a year and the worst, £671. An independent financial adviser should be able to locate the top rates for you.

◆ **Your tax position** The tax advantages of the ordinary annuity are greatest if you are a higher rate taxpayer and less, but still considerable, if you are a basic rate taxpayer. If you are a non-taxpayer, there is no advantage.

◆ **Your age and sex** The Inland Revenue decrees that a certain proportion of each ordinary annuity payment should be defined as "capital content" – in effect, a partial return of your capital – and this part of the payment is tax-free. On the taxable portion the rate is only 20% and basic rate taxpayers have no further liability. Higher rate taxpayers have to pay an extra 20% on top. The size of the capital content depends on your age at the time you buy it – some examples are shown in table 7.

Table 7
Ordinary annuities: typical amount of tax-free capital content per year on payments produced by a lump sum purchase of £10,000

Man aged 60	£466	Woman aged 60	£398
Man aged 65	£570	Woman aged 65	£482
Man aged 70	£712	Woman aged 70	£600

Note: this assumes the annuity is payable monthly in arrears and is without a guaranteed period

One gambit to consider, especially for those retiring early, is to take the cash and park it for a few years in a savings account. You can then buy an ordinary annuity, when your greater age will qualify you for higher rates and a higher tax-free capital content.

Pensions from former employers

Few people these days spend their working life with a single company; most of us are likely to have entitlements to former pension schemes tucked away somewhere. In theory, you should hear from your old employer(s) a few months before the normal retirement date of that particular scheme – which may, of course, be earlier or later than the date at which you are planning to retire.

They should explain how much you will be getting, when and any choices to be made – whether to take the tax-free cash, for instance. If you have moved house since you left a previous employer, make sure you pass on your new address.

Final salary schemes

Many "old" pensions of the final salary-type may not be all that valuable because they will not have been revalued fully (if at all) to compensate for inflation. It all depends on when you left the scheme.

If you left before 1991, only those pension rights accrued after January 1985 must be revalued, at inflation or 5% a year, whichever is less. If you left the scheme in 1991 or later, all your rights, whenever accrued, must be revalued using the same formula – inflation or 5% a year, whichever is less.

Some big private sector schemes are more generous towards the pre-1991 leavers, but they are not obliged to be. Former civil servants and other public sector workers have the advantage here. Generally, all their preserved rights are revalued in line with inflation.

There is one exception to these rules. Under a contracted out final salary scheme – one which opted out of the state earnings-related pension scheme (Serps) by promising to pay its members at least as much as Serps would have provided – that portion of preserved pension rights (known as the guaranteed minimum pension) must be revalued broadly in line with national average earnings ever since Serps began in 1978.

Money purchase schemes

The situation is more straightforward here. After you have left the company, the money invested on your behalf remains invested, so you should benefit from any growth in the fund just like current members.

Tracing pensions from former employers

Problems can arise where people have lost touch with former employers, particularly if that company has been taken over or gone out of business. But the state-run Pension Schemes Registry may be able to help.

The registry was set up in 1991 and holds details of more than 200,000 schemes (past and present). In theory, it covers pension scheme details from April 1975, but some have provided information for earlier years, so it is worth a try even if you were a member of a scheme before that date.

The service, which is free, has a success rate of more than 90% and the process usually takes around four days. You can contact the registry on 0191 225 6316 or by filling out a tracing request online at www.opra.gov.uk – obviously, the more details you can give of a former scheme, the easier it will be for the registry to find it.

Problems with company pension schemes

If you have a problem, of whatever sort, with a past or present company pension, your first port of call should be the company's pensions department. Since 1997, schemes have had an obligation under the Pensions Act 1995 to have a formal complaints procedure (known in the business as an IDR – internal disputes resolution procedure) and they must have a named person in charge of it. They must look into your problem and provide an answer within two months. If you are not satisfied, you can go to the trustees of your scheme, or with public sector schemes, to the appropriate government department.

If you are still unhappy, you can turn to the Office for the Pensions Advisory Service (Opas), an independent body whose services are free. It can be contacted either via Citizens' Advice Bureaux or through its head office (see page 178). Its website is www.opas.org.uk.

Opas manages to resolve around 90% of the cases it gets, but there is a further step for anyone unhappy with the result: they can appeal to the pensions ombudsman. The ombudsman can look into complaints relating not just to a scheme and its trustees, but also to any separate administrators or insurance company involved. There is a time limit of three years within which a complaint must be made.

The pensions ombudsman cannot act on matters relating to state pensions or to armed forces pensions where the individual is a serving member of the scheme, or on disputes of fact or law relating to most public service schemes. Nor can he act on matters which are already subject to court proceedings.

Decisions by the ombudsman are binding on both parties, subject only to an appeal on a point of law to the High Court, or the Court of Session in Scotland. If the ombudsman decides in your favour, he can award compensation if appropriate.

Finally, acting as a backstop in the complaints field, there is the Occupational Pensions Regulatory Authority (Opra) which looks after company pension schemes overall. Opra tends not to get involved in individual complaints but in cases where there has been systematic abuse by a pension scheme. If you think your scheme is breaking a fundamental rule, not just as regards you, but overall, Opra is the organisation to get in touch with. It has cracked down on a number of cases where it was alerted by individuals.

Once you initiate a complaint, in theory, you should be directed to the next stage in the procedure if you remain unsatisfied. Nevertheless, you might still find a leaflet from Opra useful. It summarises the various complaints procedures. *A Problem with Your Occupational Pension?* is available from the Opra help desk on 01273 627600 or you can find it at www.opra.gov.uk.

Tax rules on company pension schemes

Investments in pension funds are highly tax efficient. The funds themselves are almost entirely free from income and capital gains tax, while contributions attract full income tax relief. The drawback is that the pension itself is fully taxable as ordinary earned income.

These tax benefits are accompanied by rules imposing maximum limits both on the amount that can be invested and also what you can take out. The rules are, to put it mildly, complex. In practice, most people won't be affected by the maximum limits, because they both invest less and will get less on retirement, but some may run up against the rules, if, for example, they have exceptionally high earnings or they decide to take early retirement.

Set out below is a summary of these rules, but the full legislation is extremely lengthy and you should take this as a guide only.

Limits on contributions

- **Earnings cap** Anyone who joined an existing pension scheme after 1 June, 1989 (or after 14 March, 1989 if the scheme was set up after that date) is subject to the overall earnings cap. This means that income up to that level can be saved and a pension received from it. The level of the cap is increased each year, usually in line with the retail price index. The original level, in the tax year 1989-90, was £60,000; for the tax year 2001-02 it is £95,400. Employees who joined their scheme before the relevant dates are not affected by the cap.
- **Employers' contributions** There are no specific limits on employers' contributions. However, there are rules to prevent a company "over-funding" for the maximum pension allowable.
- **Employees' contributions** Employees are allowed to save up to 15% of their taxable remuneration into a company pension scheme each year. Savings made into an additional voluntary contribution (AVC) scheme are added to those made into the main scheme.

"Taxable remuneration" includes the taxable value of everything employees receive from their employer including, for example, company cars, private medical insurance and occasional bonuses. The total may be considerably more than your basic salary. There is, however, a limit in the 2001-02 tax year of £14,310 (15% of £95,400) for employees who are subject to the earnings cap.

Limits on benefits

- **The pension** The maximum pension payable is two-thirds of final remuneration, which includes the value of the taxable benefits mentioned above as well as straightforward salary, but this depends on the number of years an employee has been a member of the scheme. In addition, there can be a widow's or widower's pension of up to two-thirds of the maximum pension, and the whole lot can increase by 3% a year or inflation, whichever is greater. The scheme can also provide up to four times salary on death before retirement.
- **Length of service required to achieve maximum pension** This depends on when you joined the scheme – table 8 gives more details.

People who have a fluctuating income can, to some extent, choose which of their more recent pre-retirement years to use as the basis for their "final salary". These rules are more strict for controlling directors, who might be able to rig their salary to maximise their pension, than for ordinary employees.

The rules on maximum benefits are the same whether you have a final salary or money purchase occupational scheme. If you have a money purchase scheme (or have been saving a lot in a money purchase-type Additional Voluntary Contribution scheme) and if the investment performance has been exceptionally good, the amount you have in the fund might buy a pension greater than these limits. This problem might also arise if you take early retirement and so clock up fewer years of service than you had originally anticipated.

If this happens – which is rare but by no means unknown – the Inland Revenue steps in to stop you breaking the limits. The end result is, basically, that you lose out. In practice, a company will sometimes make an ex-gratia payment to people in this position in recognition of the fact that the pension paid is less than they "deserve". But this tends to happen only to senior executives – people who have some negotiating clout – and it must not be done on a formal basis, otherwise the taxman would forbid it.

Table 8
Length of service requirements

Years of service to normal retirement age	Maximum pension as fraction of final remuneration	
	Joined before 17 March, 1987	Joined after 17 March, 1987
1	1/60th	2/60ths
2	2/60ths	4/60ths
3	3/60ths	6/60ths
4	4/60ths	8/60ths
5	5/60ths	10/60ths
6	8/60ths	12/60ths
7	16/60ths	14/60ths
8	24/60ths	16/60ths
9	32/60ths	18/60ths
10	40/60ths	20/60ths
11-20	40/60ths	increasing by 2/60ths a year up to a maximum of 40/60ths after 20 years

The cash sum

The usual rule is you can take part of your benefits as a cash lump sum. The maximum is one-and-a-half times your final year's remuneration. This requires a certain length of service, depending on when you joined the scheme. If you have been a member for a shorter time, the maximum is less.

- **Member before March 1987** The maximum cash can be obtained after 20 years' service.
- **Joined between March 1987 and June 1989** The maximum sum can be obtained after 20 years' service, but there is an overriding cash limit of £150,000.
- **Joined after June 1989** The maximum is either two-and-a-quarter times the pension or 3/80ths of final remuneration for each year of service, whichever is greater. "Final remuneration" in this case is subject to the earnings cap, currently £95,400.

4

Saving extra for your pension

People with a company pension who can expect to retire on a full two-thirds of their final salary are few and far between. So, unless you have plenty of additional income from other sources, there is much to be said for making a last-minute push on savings to increase your income post-retirement.

As with all financial planning, there is no single right way to do this – it depends on your particular circumstances. This chapter looks at the main options for people who are already members of company pension schemes. Until 2001, the basic option for most people was to pay additional voluntary contributions, but now we have the stakeholder pension as well, which means more choice, at least for employees earning less than £30,000 a year. To decide which route is best for you, you'll need answers to the following questions:

◆ What is an additional voluntary contribution (AVC) scheme?
◆ How much can I save in one?
◆ What is a stakeholder pension?
◆ How much can I save in one?
◆ Which is better for me – AVC or stakeholder?
◆ What are the other options?

Tax benefits

AVCs and stakeholders have one important thing in common. The money you save in them qualifies for full income tax relief. If you are a basic rate taxpayer, the cost to you of saving £1,000 is, in fact, £780 and for a higher rate taxpayer, £600. Furthermore, the funds in which your money is invested are largely free of income and capital gains tax. The drawback is that the pension you get is taxed as earned income.

Additional voluntary contribution schemes

This is the classic way for people who are members of company pension schemes to save extra for their retirement. The name basically explains what it is – a scheme that allows you to make additional contributions to your pension on a voluntary basis.

As we saw in the previous chapter, under the Inland Revenue rules, companies can, in theory, provide employees with a full two-thirds pension after 20 years' service (or ten, if they joined their scheme before 1987). The practice is very different. Even a decent scheme is likely to provide a pension of two-thirds salary only after 40 years' service. This means there is plenty of scope for people to increase their pension by saving extra money in an AVC scheme.

AVCs come in two basic forms: occasionally, an employer might offer a choice of both but, usually, it will offer only one or the other.

Added years schemes

The first type is an "added years" scheme. These are available only where the employer's main pension scheme is based on final salary. Typically, a company scheme will provide 1/60th of final salary for each year of service. With this type of AVC, you literally buy more years. Although you may have worked for the company for only 20 years, you might be able to benefit from a pension of 25/60ths of final salary if you have saved enough in AVCs.

Added years schemes have one huge advantage over all other ways of saving extra for your retirement. If you get a pay increase shortly before you retire, your pension will reflect this once you retire. With other types of saving, the returns are based on the level of investment growth achieved. To take an extreme example, suppose your salary jumped from £30,000 to £40,000 in your last year of employment. That means that an added year of 1/60th final salary which you had bought through your AVC will suddenly be worth an annual pension of £666 compared to £500 without the pay rise – an increase of more than 33%. It is highly unlikely any savings scheme could match this sort of return and impossible without a huge degree of risk. But with the added years scheme, it is risk-free for the employee – it is the employer who must pick up the bill for funding it.

Most added years schemes these days are found in government or public sector schemes and, because of the way they work, they are often effectively subsidised by the employer. If you have one, it is almost certain that this will be the best way for you if to save extra for your retirement.

Money purchase schemes

The second, and more common, type of AVC is a money purchase scheme. With these, you simply save money in an investment fund and on retirement this will go to buy you an extra pension. The amount you get depends on how fast the fund has grown and annuity rates at the time you retire. In other words, they work just like the company money purchase schemes described in chapter 3.

Free-standing or in-house

Now for one more distinction. Added years schemes will only be offered by an employer, but money purchase schemes can either be offered by the employer or you can buy one independently from an insurance company – these are known as free-standing AVCs.

Free-standing AVCs are likely to have higher charges, making the in-house AVC more attractive on a straightforward value-for-money basis. Nevertheless, you might still choose a free-standing scheme if you don't like the insurance company providing the scheme for your employer or the range of funds it offers – see the section on investment considerations below.

How much can I save in an AVC?

Employees can save 15% of their taxable remuneration each year into a company pension scheme. Remuneration in this context means not just salary but the value of other taxable benefits such as a company car, private medical insurance and so on.

Most company pension schemes require some contribution from employees – typically, between 2% and 6%. So an employee contributing 4% to his main company scheme can save an extra 11% through an AVC. In some cases, the amount he can save may be higher still, because company schemes usually base their contribution percentages on basic pay only, ignoring taxable extras.

There is one "but", however. As we saw in chapter 3, the Inland Revenue imposes limits on the amount of pension you can take from a company scheme and these depend on the number of years you have worked for the company – see table 8 on page 41.

It is not common but a few people do save too much in their AVCs, and end up with a fund that would buy them a bigger pension than they are entitled to get under these rules. They may simply have saved too much or their AVC fund may have grown faster than expected. Or they may have decided to take early retirement so don't clock up the number of years' service they were expecting. In this case, the surplus investment is returned, but only after the taxman has deducted 32% (basic rate tax plus 10%). Higher rate taxpayers must then hand over a further 18%.

There are still more Inland Revenue rules on how the benefits from an AVC fund may be taken on retirement and these differ according to when you joined your company scheme and started making AVC payments.

- **Before 8 April, 1987** Benefits can be taken either as cash (within the overall limits of one-and-a-half times salary, depending on the length of service) or as additional pension.
- **After 8 April, 1987 and before 14 March, 1989** Benefits must be taken as pension – so any cash entitlement must come from the main company scheme.
- **After 14 March, 1989** For schemes set up after this date, or for people who joined existing schemes after 1 June 1989, the restriction is the same as for April 1987 to March 1989, but with the additional constraint of the earnings cap, which limits the maximum final salary that can be taken into account (see page 39).

Bill Langland is 57 and will be retiring in three years. His company scheme will provide a pension at retirement of one-third of his final salary, currently £40,000. This is non-contributory. He decides to save the maximum possible in an AVC scheme to increase his pension.

AVC savings: 15% of £40,000	£6,000
Total invested over three years	£18,000
Total net cost of AVCs (after 40% tax relief)	£10,800
Value of AVC fund at retirement	£19,861
Which buys an additional gross pension of	£1,390

This table assumes, for convenience, that Langland's salary will not increase between now and retirement. It also assumes the AVC fund will earn 5% a year while it is invested.

The AVC pension figure assumes Langland is married, that his wife is the same age and includes a widow's pension of two-thirds. A single man of 60 could buy a pension of about £1,575 gross for the same amount.

Langland has qualified for income tax relief at 40% on the full AVC saving and, as he will be paying only basic rate tax on retirement, he has done especially well, achieving a net income for life of £1,084 in return for a total outlay of £10,800. If he had received only basic rate relief on his AVC savings, at 22%, the figures would be less impressive, but still good. The total net cost of his AVCs would have been £14,040 rather than £10,800.

The stakeholder alternative

Stakeholder pension plans became available in 2001. They were introduced to encourage people without a company scheme to start saving for retirement but the rules allow other people to invest as well. The only people who cannot invest in a stakeholder plan are members of a company scheme who are earning more than £30,000 a year, controlling directors of a company (however little they earn) and anyone over the age of 75. Controlling directors are defined as directors who, in common with immediate members of their family, control 20% or more of a company's shares.

What is it?

A stakeholder plan is a money purchase scheme and works in the same way as a money purchase company pension or AVC scheme. Cash is invested in a fund and at retirement most of it must be used to buy an annuity.

How much can you invest in a stakeholder?

Except for people in one of the forbidden categories above, anyone can save up to £3,600 a year. If you don't have any sort of company pension, you may be able to invest more – this is dealt with in the following chapter.

The situation with regard to members of company schemes who are earning about £30,000 is a little complicated. The government wants to ensure that employees who are eligible to save in a stakeholder scheme one year are not barred the very next year, just because their pay has crept over £30,000. To do this, it invented the concept of "base years". You will be allowed to look back over the previous five years and if, in any one of these, you earned less than £30,000, you will be eligible to contribute to stakeholder plan in the current tax year.

Because this system has only just come into being, there is only one base year available so far – the current tax year, 2001-02. Next tax year, 2002-03, we will have two years, in the following tax year three and so on. So if, for instance, you earn less than £30,000 in 2001-02 but more in 2002-03, you will still be able to save in a stakeholder plan in 2002-03 and for the subsequent three years.

AVC or stakeholder: which is best?

If you're lucky enough to have an added-years AVC available, it is likely to provide the best value. But if your company offers only a money purchase AVC, does it matter whether you go for the AVC or stakeholder, given that the two work in basically the same way? The answer is that it might. Here are the things you have to look out for:

Charges

Providers of stakeholder plans cannot charge more than 1% a year for setting up and running their schemes. Charges on AVC schemes vary. Some in-house schemes might be subsidised by the employer, so that the charges are less. Some free-standing AVCs might charge a good bit more.

Employer's contribution

Some employers will match any contributions an employee makes to an in-house AVC scheme. It's rare but does happen – if yours is a scheme like this, it's worth joining.

Tax-free cash

With a stakeholder, you can take 25% of the pension fund as tax-free cash on retirement. With an AVC, most people must take their fund in the form of an added pension, with any cash sum coming out of the main company scheme.

Most people like the idea of taking the cash, making the stakeholder the more attractive option.

Maximum limits

With an AVC scheme, there are rules not just about the maximum you can save (15% of salary) but also about the maximum amount you can take out. If you save too much in an AVC, part of the fund will be returned to you, after a hefty tax charge. Stakeholder is different. There are no limits on how much you can take out on retirement. This makes it the better option.

Investment choice

In-house AVC schemes might offer a couple of funds for employees to choose between: perhaps a managed fund and a lower-risk fixed-interest and cash fund. Stakeholder plans may offer a greater investment choice.

If you are just a few years off retirement, this is probably not the time to be taking big investment risks. If stock markets tumbled just before you retired, your pension would suffer. There are ways round this, as we shall see in chapter 6 on the different types of annuity available and their alternatives. But basically, if you expect to be on a fairly tight budget after retirement and don't have huge amounts of other resources, you should stick to a cash or fixed-interest fund.

What are the other options?

Stakeholder and AVC plans are the obvious choices for someone wanting to make last-minute savings to increase their retirement income, but they do have one limitation: you are forced to take the bulk of the money you have saved in the form of a regular income rather than a lump sum.

This is a feature of pension plans that has become increasingly unpopular with many people who would rather have full access to their capital, either to spend or to leave to their heirs. The rules have been eased somewhat in that you do not have to start taking the pension until age 75, and if you die before then, the money in the fund can be left to your heirs. But this is not a lot of help if you live longer – as most people do these days. Despite a vociferous campaign to extend the age to 80, or to abolish it completely, it looks for the moment as if the government has decided against making any change.

If this is important to you, you won't want to save in either an AVC or a stakeholder scheme. The main alternative is an individual savings account (Isa).

What can Isas offer?

An Isa is basically a tax-free wrapper around another savings product – it can be a building society account or a unit or investment trust, for example. They are described in more detail in chapters 10 and 11.

AVC, stakeholder or Isa – how do I choose?

The most important decision is to start making those savings; which vehicle you choose is of less importance. But here are a few pointers:

- If you want cash and are not concerned about an income, choose an Isa.
- If your sole aim is to increase retirement income, choose an in-house AVC or a stakeholder, if you are eligible.
- If you would like to have a cash lump sum as well as a retirement income, choose a stakeholder in preference to an AVC as this increases your entitlement to cash.
- If your tax rate is high now, but you expect it to drop once you retire, choose an AVC or stakeholder. You will get the benefit of tax relief on your contributions at the higher rate, while the income you withdraw after retirement will be taxed at a lower rate.

Lateral thinking

Sometimes it pays to think laterally in financial planning. Take the example of a married couple where the husband works and the wife does not and has no income of her own (it could, of course, be the other way round).

His income is subject to basic rate tax, which he will still be paying on the top slice of his pension when he retires. She does not have any pension of her own, which means that her tax-free personal allowance will not be used.

Non-earners are also allowed to save up to £3,600 a year in stakeholder plan and they too get tax relief on their contributions – to invest £3,600 they actually have to save £2,808 net.

By taking out the stakeholder in his wife's name, they get the benefit of tax relief on the way in, while the income from the pension it produces after retirement will – because it belongs to his wife – be tax-free.

There is one other point to note. Married men usually buy a joint life pension, which incorporates a widow's pension, usually payable at half or two-thirds of the full level. This is sensible, given that women tend to outlive their husbands. But if the additional stakeholder pension is in the wife's name, it can be taken out on a single life basis, which means the annuity rate may well be higher. If, in fact, she dies first, this means he will have to make do without her pension – but he will continue to get 100% of the pension from his company scheme, whereas if he dies first, his company pension will pay her a widow's pension of only a half or two-thirds. The table shows how the sums work out.

Table 9
Using a stakeholder plan for extra pension income

	Husband	Wife
Net stakeholder investment of £2,808 for five years		
Value of fund after five years*	£20,279	£20,279
Which provides a tax-free cash sum of	£5,070	£5,070
Plus a gross pension of**	£1,034	£1,095
Pension after tax	£807	£1,095

*Assuming the underlying fund grows at 4% a year after charges
**Husband's pension is joint life with two-thirds widow's pension, wife's pension is single life (with no widower's pension). Both are level pensions, guaranteed for five years, payable monthly in arrears. Husband and wife are both aged 60 on retirement

Source: Best Invest

The open market option

Whether you are saving through an AVC or a stakeholder plan, you have complete freedom once you come to retirement to take the fund you have accumulated to another company to buy the pension annuity. It is invariably worth shopping around at this point. Annuity rates vary widely between companies and you might be able to increase your income by 10% or more – and you have only this one chance to make the best of it, as once the annuity has been purchased, you are stuck with it for life and cannot swap to another provider.

There are a number of issues involved and choices to be made, when it comes to annuities. Chapter 6 goes into these in detail.

5

Individual pensions

If you have not been able to join a company pension scheme, then – I hope – you will have some form of individual arrangement. Most likely, you will have what is known as a personal pension; if you started saving before 1988 you will probably have a retirement annuity plan (Rap), also known as a section 226 scheme, and if you started a new scheme in the last year, you may well have a stakeholder pension. This chapter covers:

◆ Individual pensions: what they are and how they work
◆ Which scheme you should choose
◆ Self-invested pensions
◆ Opportunities for last-minute saving
◆ Countdown to retirement – dealing with investment risk
◆ Where to find out more

The rules

All three types of plan are money purchase schemes. This means that your savings are invested in one or more investment funds and must at some point be turned into a pension annuity giving you an annual income for life. The amount of income you will get depends on:

◆ How much you have saved
◆ How well the investments have performed
◆ Annuity rates at the time you take the income

All forms of individual pension savings have big tax breaks, but there are also strict rules on how you can take the money out. Personal and stakeholder pensions follow the same rules but Raps are slightly different.

With all three, the pension funds are totally free from capital gains tax and largely free from income tax. Up to certain limits, your premiums qualify for tax relief at your marginal tax rate. And with all three, you must turn most of your fund into an annuity, currently by no later than age 75. You do not have to have retired before you take the pension – and you do not have to take it immediately after you retire either.

Late last year, the government announced that it was to review this age limit, which has been unpopular with many savers, and it is possible that this may change although, at present, it looks unlikely. The annuity itself is all taxed as earned income. The maximum you can put into the pension differs according to which plan you have.

Unlike company pension schemes, there are no limits on how much pension you can take out of the scheme. If you have saved the maximum amounts, and your investments have performed spectacularly well, you could retire on a higher pension than your pre-retirement earnings – at least in theory.

You are allowed to take out some of your pension fund as a cash sum on retirement, the amount depending on which plan you have.

Stakeholder

Anyone – whether earning or not – can save up to £3,600 a year gross into a stakeholder plan (but see page 47). This means you can do it if you have never worked, or even after you have retired if you want to increase your post-retirement income. The premiums are paid net of tax relief, which means the maximum net contribution is £2,808 a year. Even if you don't pay tax, you benefit from the relief.

If you have earnings which are not covered by some other form of pension, you may be able to save more, depending on how much they are – see table 10. High earners are limited as to the maximum they can put in by the "pensions cap". You can take your pension at any age between 50 and 75. You can take up to 25% of the fund as tax-free cash on retirement.

Personal pensions

You can save in a personal pension only in respect of earnings which are not covered under some other pension scheme. The amount you can

Individual pensions

save depends on your age and your earnings – see table 10. High earners are limited as to the maximum they can put in by the pensions cap. You can take your pension at any age between 50 and 75. You can take up to 25% of the pension fund as tax-free cash on retirement.

Raps

You can save in a Rap only if you took out the plan before 1988, which is when they were superseded by personal pensions. The amounts you can save depend on your age and your earnings. For most people, the limits are lower than with a personal or stakeholder pension, but high earners fare better, because they are not subject to the pensions cap. You can take your pension at any age between 60 and 75.

You can take a tax-free cash sum equal to three times the remaining annuity at retirement. As annuity rates are low these days, the resulting figure is likely to be less than 25%, but it may be possible to convert your Rap into a personal pension immediately before retirement so you can benefit from the higher figure. Get professional advice before you do so, in case you lose other benefits of the Rap. Chapter 6 gives more details.

Table 10
Maximum annual savings allowed in individual pensions

	Stakeholder and personal pensions		Rap	
Age on 6 April	Percentage of earnings	Overall maximum	% of earnings	Overall maximum
35 or less	17.5%	£16,695	17.5%	-
36-45	20%	£19,080	17.5%	-
46-50	25%	£23,850	17.5%	-
51-55	30%	£28,620	20%	-
56-60	35%	£33,390	22.5%	-
61-74	40%	£38,160	27.5%	-

Note: savings of up to £3,600 a year gross can be made into stakeholder even if you have no earnings

The pensions cap prevents people who started saving in a pension plan after 1988-89 using earnings in excess of a certain figure to save for a pension. The cap is revalued each year, usually in line with price inflation. In 2001-02, it is £95,400.

Which plan do you choose?

You probably already have at least one type of plan. But if you are still saving for your retirement, you do not have to stick with the one you have. Here are some pointers as to which plan to choose:

- If you are a high earner, and you already have a Rap, you may be able to save more in it than in the other two schemes because the pensions cap does not apply. The cross-over point depends on your age. If you are over 61, for example, then in the 2001-02 tax year, you will be able to save more in the Rap if your earnings exceed £138,763. If you do not already have a Rap, you cannot start one now.
- If you have no earnings, you must choose a stakeholder plan, as this is the only one that allows this.
- If you are not liable to tax on your earnings, or to tax at only the 10% rate, choose a stakeholder, as this is the only scheme which provides automatic basic rate relief (at 22%) on premiums.
- If your current plan (Rap or personal) provides a guaranteed annuity rate which applies to any new savings you put in, stick with this. The guaranteed rate is likely to be much higher than those available on the open market – see chapter 6 for details.

Charges

The government has set strict rules on the charges and other terms that pension companies are allowed to impose on stakeholder plans. They cannot charge more than 1% a year and the minimum saving must be no more than £20 a month. There must be no penalties for increasing or reducing your savings or for transferring to another provider.

These rules may mean that a stakeholder is cheaper than your current plan, but not necessarily. Some old personal and Rap schemes imposed a big charge up-front, followed by very low annual management fees. If you have one of these, it may be cheaper to stick with it than to start a stakeholder plan now.

New personal pension charges tend to be broadly the same as for stakeholders.

Self-invested personal pensions (Sipps)

Sipps are a special form of personal pension aimed at the wealthy. With most schemes, your money is invested in one or a range of investment funds, managed by a single company. A Sipp is basically a "shell" pension plan, where you or your adviser can choose what investments to have. You can hire and fire your own investment managers.

Sipps are suitable only for those with significant sums in their fund, say £200,000-plus, as initial charges are higher than for conventional schemes. One of their main roles is when the plan is used for income drawdown after retirement – see chapter 6 for details.

Last-minute savings

Now that you are within sight of retirement, you should have a fair idea of how much your pension will be. Your pension provider will give you a quotation based on likely fund growth between now and retirement and current annuity rates. But bear in mind that it is only an estimate, not a guarantee.

If you would like more income in retirement, you will have to save extra now. It may even be worth saving in a pension fund one day and taking it out as a pension more or less the next (although given the state of administration in many large companies, it would be prudent to allow a good few weeks for the operation).

If you are saving shortly before your retirement, you should not take too great an investment risk. Choose a fixed-interest or cash fund, or perhaps a managed fund which is invested cautiously.

Is it worth doing? If your overriding need is for extra income, the answer is definitely yes. The only exception is if your expected retirement income (including state pensions) is so low that the minimum income guarantee would provide more than your savings. In that case, you should think carefully before going ahead.

If you simply want more money after retirement, but would like some of this in the form of a lump sum rather than a regular income, the answer is maybe. Consider putting the money in an individual savings account (Isa) instead, because all the savings can be withdrawn as capital.

But remember, savings made into an Isa do not qualify for income tax relief, whereas those into a pension do. Because of this, one of the biggest benefits appears if you expect to drop down a tax band after retirement, as the following example shows.

Individual pensions

Tom Hardy is 65 and planning to retire shortly. He puts £10,000 into a personal or stakeholder pension plan and, because he is a 40% taxpayer, receives back £4,000 in the form of tax relief. He immediately starts drawing his pension, taking out 25% of the total gross fund in cash – another £2,500. He buys a level, joint life annuity (reducing by one third after his death) which pays an income for life of £540. After basic rate tax this is £421.20. It has cost him just £3,500 to provide this annual income – an effective yield of 12% after tax.

You can achieve equally good results if you are a basic rate taxpayer now and expect to be liable for no tax after retirement, or, using a stakeholder, if you are a non-taxpayer now and expect to remain so after retirement. Thanks to stakeholder rules, non-taxpayers still get basic rate relief on pension contributions.

If you are married and your spouse is in this position, it will be worth channelling extra pension savings into a stakeholder plan in their name, rather than taking out your own, if you expect to be paying tax at the same rate after retirement. An example of this is shown in chapter 4.

If you do not expect to drop a tax band after retirement, the playing field does not slope as much. Pensions still provide a benefit over Isas, because you can take out the tax-free cash, but the sums are more modest.

Countdown to retirement: investment risk

We mentioned above that if you are investing new money shortly before retirement, you should not take too great an investment risk. But this also applies to money you already have invested. Once you are within five years, say, of your expected retirement age, you should take a close look at exactly where your money is invested and consider whether you should switch to a more cautious fund. Many people have with-profits pension funds and, because these are fairly cautiously managed, with reserves held back to smooth out performance in bad years, you may decide to leave them where they are. But if your money is invested wholly in equity funds, it may be wise to think of switching into fixed interest some time before retirement – possibly at a rate of 20% a year for the five years prior to retirement.

This may not be necessary. The next chapter deals with the ways in which you can take an income from your pension fund after retirement. The most common is to use a fixed-interest annuity, which involves selling all the holdings in your pension fund. But there are alternatives which mean your pension fund can remain invested in equities after your retirement, so you are not running the risk of being forced to cash in all your investments when stock markets have fallen.

Where to find out more

There is plenty of information on personal and stakeholder pensions. The Financial Services Authority's website, at www.fsa.gov.uk, has a large section on stakeholder pensions, including an interactive decision tree which allows you to enter personal details and which will suggest whether a stakeholder is appropriate for you and provide a list of schemes which would be suitable.

The Office for the Pensions Advisory Service (Opas) runs a stakeholder helpline on 0845 601 2923 and the Department of Work and Pensions has a pensions information line on 0845 731 3233. The government also publishes a number of booklets including *Stakeholder Pensions – Your Guide*.

If you want an overall review of your finances, however, or if you have complex arrangements, it is best to get professional advice from an independent financial adviser.

6

The annuity choice

People with final salary company pension schemes, whose AVC scheme is also of the added years variety, can skip this chapter. For everyone else, whether they have a company money purchase scheme, a personal pension, retirement annuity, stakeholder plan or a money purchase AVC, this is the big one. It's possible that reading this could mean you enjoy an income 10% higher for the rest of your life than you would have done otherwise. It covers:

- How annuities work
- When you should buy one
- Whether you should take the cash lump sum
- Fixed-interest annuities
- With-profits and unit-linked annuities
- Phased retirement
- Income drawdown plans

How annuities work

An annuity is an income for life, paid by an insurance company in return for a lump sum. Anyone with savings in a pension plan must use most of that money to buy an annuity no later than age 75. There is a great deal of pressure on the government to abolish this requirement and it has announced a review, but these rules remain in place for now.

Pension annuities are taxed as earned income – unlike purchased life annuities which are taxed more lightly. Basic rate tax is usually deducted at source, unless you are a non-taxpayer or a 10% taxpayer, in which case it may be paid gross. Higher rate taxpayers must declare the income on their tax return and pay the extra due.

An annuity is paid for the whole of your life, however long (or short) that might be. But there is not usually any return of capital after your death, even if you die just after buying one. The insurance company's "profit" goes to subsidise the income of those who live longer than average.

There are numerous variations on the basic concept of an annuity and a lot of work is going into devising yet more sophisticated products.

When should you buy one?

Personal pension planholders (which includes people with stakeholder pensions) have great leeway under Inland Revenue rules as to when they must buy an annuity: they can do so at any age between 50 and 75 (and do not have to retire before buying). Retirement annuity plans (Raps) allow annuities to be bought from age 60 and, again, no later than age 75. Those with a money purchase AVC plan will generally buy their annuity at the time they retire, although they need not always do so.

If you continue working after your formal retirement date, or have other sources of income, or if the alternative of income drawdown (see page 72) is suitable for you, it may be difficult to work out the best time to buy the annuity. These are some factors to bear in mind when making that decision:

Life expectancy

If you expect to live longer than the average, buy an annuity earlier rather than later. As life expectancy in general improves, annuity rates will fall.

Mortality drag

Although annuity rates are higher the older you are when you buy one, they do not increase by as much as you would expect, thanks to the pattern of life expectancy which you can see in tables 1 and 2 in the introduction. The rate you get when you buy one is based on the average life expectancy for your age at that point. As table 1 shows, at 60, an average man will live until he is nearly 78, but a 70-year-old man will, on average, live till he is 81. The later you leave buying one, the less you will benefit from the subsidy effect of those who die early. Your pension fund would have to grow that much faster to counteract this effect, which is called the mortality drag.

State of health

The longest-lived benefit most from an annuity, but what of those in poor health, who do not expect to make old bones? If you are confident of dying before age 75, you might consider delaying purchase – if you can afford it – so that your heirs can inherit the full value of your pension fund (less tax). But then, you might survive. What you should probably be considering is an impaired life annuity, which will pay out a higher income in recognition of your shorter life expectancy – see page 67.

What happens when you decide to retire?

The pension provider with whom you have built up your fund will offer you an annuity and possibly several choices. One of these concerns the lump sum.

Stakeholder and personal pension planholders can take up to 25% of their total fund as a tax-free cash sum or they can opt for the whole amount to be used to pay an income.

Retirement annuity plan (Rap) holders are allowed to take a cash sum equal to three times the maximum allowable residual annuity. The end result is likely to be less than 25% of the total fund – it depends on annuity rates and your age at the time you retire. At current annuity rates, a man retiring at 65 could get a maximum cash sum of just over 21% of the total fund, 19% if he retired at 60. A woman could get 19% of the fund at age 65 and 17.4% at 60.

If you want to take the absolute maximum as cash and you have a Rap, see an independent adviser about transferring the fund to a personal pension plan immediately before you buy the annuity. You will then be able to take the full 25% as cash. There may be charges, but these can be small.

Those with AVC funds are not allowed to take a lump sum unless they started saving before April 1987.

Should you take the cash lump sum?

Most people do. You might want to spend it having fun or perhaps want some capital to leave to your heirs.

Even if you really need the income, it will probably be better to take the cash and buy an ordinary, purchased life annuity rather than a pension annuity. This is because purchased life annuities are taxed more lightly, so while their rates are often lower, you will end up with a higher net income. An example of how this works is given on page 35. Get independent advice at this stage to ensure you are getting the best rate.

Open market option

Your next choice is whether to take the annuity offered by your pension provider. The golden rule is: not without getting independent advice first. Unless your policy incorporates a guaranteed annuity rate (see page 66) there is a strong likelihood that you will do better by going elsewhere. You are entitled to take your fund and buy an annuity from whatever company is offering the best rates.

Fixed-interest annuities

These are the main type of annuity. They come in three guises:
- **Level annuities** These will pay the same sum every year until you die, no matter what happens to inflation, interest rates or general investment conditions.
- **Escalating annuities** These pay a steadily increasing income at a rate determined in advance. Typically, it might increase at 3% or 5% a year.
- **Index-linked annuities** These pay an income which is guaranteed to increase in line with inflation each year.

The second and third options are much more expensive than the first and you would have to live for many years before you made a "profit" by choosing one of these over the level pension. The majority of people prefer not to, or more likely cannot afford to, choose them. Examples of the different rates are shown in table 11.

Table 11
Pension annuity rates for a purchase price of £10,000

	Level, no guarantee	Level, 5yr guarantee	Increasing at 5% a year*	Inflation linked*
Single Life				
Man 60	£762	£758	£448	£549
Man 65	£862	£854	£549	£650
Man 70	£1,001	£982	£688	£788
Woman 60	£684	£683	£371	£470
Woman 65	£754	£750	£442	£542
Woman 70	£850	£843	£540	£639
Joint lives, including two-thirds widow's pension				
Man 60/Woman 55	£663	£661	£347	£448
Man 65/Woman 60	£724	£721	£410	£511
Man 70/Woman 65	£808	£802	£495	£595

*Without guaranteed period

Source: Moneyfacts

The rates in the above example were taken from a single company, which was not necessarily the most competitive for all ages. To show the extent to which rates can differ, the very best for a single man aged 65, without a guaranteed period, was £879 if he was in good health, or £932 for a smoker or if he was in poor health, while the lowest on offer was £797.

Choosing a level annuity is a gamble. If inflation takes off, the real value of your pension income will decline year by year. There is no satisfactory solution to this – you simply have to decide whether you are prepared to take that risk for the sake of a much higher income now. One factor is that, in the early years of retirement, you will presumably still be living an active life, travelling and spending money, whereas later on, spending needs tend to be less.

Other choices to be made

Joint or single life

A single life annuity normally stops on your death. If you are married or living with someone, you need the joint life option, where income continues until the second death.

With joint life annuities, if the planholder's partner is the first to die, the income continues at the original rate. However, if the planholder dies first, income may be payable at a reduced rate, depending on what was chosen at the outset. You can choose a pension that continues at half, two-thirds or the original level.

These options tend to cost more than a single life annuity – unless your partner is much older than yourself and in poor health. There might be some circumstances in which you would be better taking a single life annuity even though you are married. If you both have a good pension income, and if you have a guaranteed rate built into your policy which applies only if a single life annuity is taken, it could be worth taking that option, despite the risk. But you should seek independent advice before deciding.

Income frequency

Annuities can be paid monthly, sometimes quarterly or even annually. You can choose to be paid in advance or in arrears. The longer you are prepared to wait for the money, the higher the payments will be.

Guaranteed period

All annuities are paid for as long as you live, but it is possible to choose one with a guaranteed period which means it will be paid during the term, even if you die. You can usually choose a period of five or ten years. For someone retiring relatively young, the cost of taking an annuity with a five-year guaranteed period is very low compared to an annuity with no guaranteed period at all, but the older you are, the more expensive it will be.

Guaranteed annuity rates

In the 1970s and 1980s, many self-employed pension plans were sold with guaranteed annuity rates. It meant that planholders had at least some certainty when they retired. In those days, gilt yields – on which annuity rates depend – were much higher, so the rates offered by these plans are much higher than you can obtain today on the open market.

These guarantees have not been good news for the life companies, most notably Equitable Life whose problems have been well publicised. Other companies are still honouring their guaranteed rates, but they are sticking closely to the precise terms of the contract. In some cases, the guarantee is given only for a single life, level annuity without escalation. If you are married, you may simply have to forgo that rate, although as noted above, if both of you have a good pension in your own right, it may pay to take it.

It is also likely that the rate is guaranteed only if you retire at a particular date – say, on your 65th birthday. You should do your best to keep to this date.

Impaired life annuities

If you are in poor health, get professional advice to see whether it is worth trying for an "impaired life" annuity. The lower your life expectancy, the higher the rate may be, although if you have a younger partner in good health, the improvement on a joint life annuity may be small.

Impaired life annuities may be available not just to those who are suffering from a serious illness, but also to people whose work involved heavy manual labour and to smokers. As an example, a single man of 60 could, at the time of writing, get an annuity of £932 a year for a purchase price of £10,000 if he was a regular smoker, compared with £862 for non-smokers. A single woman of 60 could get an annuity of £734 a year for the same purchase price, compared with £684 as a non-smoker. You can, of course, give up as soon as you have secured the annuity – you will still get the higher payments as long as you live.

Why are annuity rates so low?

The immediate reaction of many people when they get their first annuity quotation from their pension provider is that rates seem extremely low, scarcely better than they could get by putting the money in a building society. But this is not because annuity providers are making huge profits. To offer annuities, they must buy government securities (gilts), which provide a reliable stream of income. In the early 1980s, gilt yields were as high as 15%; today, they are more like 5% or even lower. Part of each annuity payment is, in effect, the return of your capital as you get back none when you die. This is why annuity rates are higher than gilt yields. The other reason rates are so low is that people tend to live a lot longer than they used to, so the capital must be spread a great deal more thinly.

Many people wonder why they cannot simply invest the capital themselves, live off the interest and top it up with small withdrawals of capital. The ultimate reason is that the law won't allow them to – but even if it did, it is not as straightforward a process as it might seem. How long are you going to live? How much capital could you withdraw each year without running out? The more you withdraw, the less remains invested to provide interest, which means you would have to withdraw yet more the following year, and so on. Imagine living to 85 and realising that you are going to run out of capital next year – or worse, leaving your widow or widower in that situation.

Much has been written in the press about the dreadful value provided by annuities and this has spurred the industry on to devise other, in certain respects more attractive, vehicles, which are described below. But not all the press coverage has been fair or fully considered. For many – perhaps even the majority of – people retiring today with relatively limited pension funds, a straightforward fixed-interest annuity is still the best way to provide a reliable income until they die.

With-profits and unit-linked annuities

With these annuities, the amount paid out depends partly on interest rates and partly on the performance of an underlying investment fund. If the investment performs well, payments should rise over the years and you will do better overall than if you had chosen a fixed-interest annuity. But there is an investment risk.

At the outset, the annuitant specifies a level of income that he or she wants from the annuity. This requires that investment growth reaches a target level during that year. Assuming it succeeds, they will get the income specified; if not, their income will drop. These annuities are, therefore, not suitable for people operating on tight budgets, where the annuity is their main source of income.

Buyers can help themselves by choosing a reasonably modest starting income. In the longer-term past, these annuities have proved a rewarding choice – as investment returns have been higher than the target rate, people have experienced a rising income. But over the past couple of years, as the stock market has gone into reverse, many people who chose such an annuity will now be experiencing a drop in income.

The choice of risks

While, clearly, there are risks involved in choosing this type of annuity, there is another sense it in which such a choice is actually less risky than a fixed-interest annuity. In the period up to retirement, a pension fund is generally invested largely in equities, which is then, on a single day, turned into an annuity. The level of income you receive for the rest of your life depends on the value of your fund and the level of interest rates on the day of retirement. If the stock market falls the day before, and you choose a fixed-interest annuity, your income will be less than it would have been had you retired earlier. But if you choose a with-profits or unit-linked annuity, your fund is still exposed to the stock market and you will benefit when it recovers.

Who do with-profits and unit-linked annuities suit?

As indicated above, these are not the best choice for people with limited funds, relying solely, or largely, on their pension to meet living expenses after retirement – they are simply too risky. But if you have other reliable sources of income, they may well play a part, especially if you are retiring early and need some form of inflation-proofing for your income. They cannot, of course, guarantee that the income they produce will rise in line with inflation, but there is a good chance that it will over the long term, just as company profits and dividends tend to rise over the years.

Another instance where they may be considered is if you have a company pension scheme and have built up an AVC fund which must be turned into an annuity (this is the case for anyone who started contributing to their AVC after April 1987). Because the AVC pension may be the icing on the cake, you might be able to afford the greater risk they entail.

A word of warning: people with company schemes are limited as to the total pension they may take, depending on their number of years' service. It is possible, in some circumstances, that if a with-profits or unit-linked AVC performed exceptionally well, they could breach those limits – but they would not be able to draw the extra income.

Mixing annuities

With most pension schemes you do not have to buy a single annuity, although if your total pension fund is not that large, you may come up against minimum investment requirements. Suppose, however, you have a pension fund worth £300,000. You could put £100,000, maybe, into a fixed-interest annuity and the balance in a with-profits or unit-linked one.

Phased retirement and staggered vesting

These are two popular catchphrases in the pensions industry. Both refer to something that self-employed people have been doing in an informal way for years. Instead of turning all their pension policies into annuities in one go, they have phased them in over a number of years as they wind down from work. As their working income falls, they can gradually build up their pension income.

This, of course, assumes that people have more than one policy. You probably do, even if you are not aware of it, as these days, companies generally "segment" their pension policies into many small parts. This segmentation is notional in a sense, as it makes no difference to the way the policy is invested or run – its purpose is purely to allow such phasing to take place. As long as people obey the overall age limits on retirement – between 50 and 75 with a personal or stakeholder pension – they can phase them in at any time.

This informal phasing has now been taken a step further with the concept of staggered vesting. This requires pensions policies to be segmented into 100 or more parts and each year a certain number are cashed in to provide that year's income, leaving the rest to benefit from future growth. The scheme makes use of the 25% tax-free cash entitlement from each policy to produce the first slice of that year's income. Table 12 shows how it might work in practice.

Table 12:
Staggered vesting: how it might work

Pension fund: £300,000. Target yearly income: £20,000

Age	Starting fund	Amount encashed	Tax-free cash	Annuity payment	Total income	Remaining fund
60	£300,000	£65,400	£16,350	£3,650	£20,000	£235,000
61	£235,000	£52,100	£13,025	£7,000	£20,025	£192,000
62	£192,000	£41,600	£10,400	£9,600	£20,000	£160,000
63	£160,000	£32,900	£8,225	£11,770	£19,995	£135,000
64	£135,000	£25,700	£6,425	£13,560	£19,985	£116,000
and so on until...						
73	£81,700	£2,510	£628	£19,370	£19,998	£84,300
74	£84,300	£1,330	£333	£19,600	£19,933	£88,300
75	£88,300*					

*This will provide tax-free cash of £22,000 plus an additional pension of £8,650 a year, alongside the continuing pension of £19,600.

The table assumes level annuity payments and annual growth at 7% on investments remaining within the fund. If they grew more slowly, income would diminish with age. Remember that each year's annuity payments are added to those being made from the annuities started up in earlier years. Income payments are shown before tax.

Note: the way this particular scheme has been constructed gives rise to a big leap in income from age 75. It would be possible, by cashing in more segments in the earlier years, to have a smoother progression, but the thinking behind it is to build in a bit of a safety net in case investments do not grow steadily at the 7% forecasted. This is a very sensible precaution, because there can be no guarantees.

Source: Clerical Medical

You should take this table with a pinch of salt, because it is very unlikely that investments will produce steady 7% growth over the year. This is the biggest drawback of the scheme. If growth faltered, all these neat assumptions would be thrown into disarray. Two further points should be borne in mind: this scheme depends on taking the 25% cash entitlement each year to provide part of the income, which means you never get your hands on one big cash sum at retirement. And it is suitable only for those who have substantial money in their pension fund –

maybe upwards of £200,000. Finally, you must remember that the clock stops at age 75. At this point, as the law currently stands, you are required to turn the remaining fund into an annuity.

On the plus side, staggered vesting allows people to draw a pension income from an early age without giving up all potential for investment growth. It avoids having to cash in the lot on a particular day. It has advantages, too, in the event of death before age 75 as the balance of the fund (the portion that has not yet been turned into annuities) can be inherited by your heirs. With annuities, remember, while the income is guaranteed for life, no capital is repayable on death.

Income drawdown plans

Income drawdown plans allow people to delay turning any of their pension fund into an annuity until age 75. Instead, they can draw an income directly from the fund, at a level to suit themselves, although there are legal maximum and minimum levels. If you want to take the 25% cash sum, you must do so when you start the income drawdown.

Maximum and minimum income

The maximum amount you can withdraw is equivalent to that produced by a fixed-interest annuity for someone of your age. The minimum is 35% of the maximum. These levels are reviewed every three years. Your pension fund is revalued and if it has grown, both maximum and minimum levels will rise, while if it has fallen in value, the levels may fall.

The advantages

There are three main advantages to income drawdown. The first is that your fund can benefit from future investment growth. The second is that if you die before age 75, most of the remaining capital can be passed to your heirs, less a tax charge of 34%. If there is a widow or widower, income withdrawal can continue until either the survivor reaches 75 or the planholder would have been 75, if this is earlier. Alternatively, it can be turned into an annuity straight away. Finally, the scheme is flexible, allowing you (within the overall limits) to vary the amount of income you take each year, which may be useful if you have other income coming in from time to time.

The disadvantages

As with phased retirement and staggered vesting, the main disadvantage is that you continue taking an investment risk with your fund. If it falls in value, the amount of income you can take will fall as well, as many people are learning to their cost. And if the fund falls below a certain level at any age (even if well before 75) it must be turned into an annuity straight away – you have no choice in the matter.

For this reason, it is probably wise not to take the maximum income from the start, because this means taking greater risks with the remaining fund.

Many experts suggest that people set up a self-invested personal pension (Sipp) when they start a drawdown scheme. This involves paying a fee to a pension company which will set up a "shell" scheme. You, or your adviser, will be able to choose from different investment managers, to split it between several, and – if need be – ditch one later in favour of another if performance is poor.

Because of the risk involved, income drawdown schemes are suitable only for those with big pension funds. Many independent advisers suggest you should have at least £200,000 or even £500,000 before considering it. The only exception would be if you already have a decent pension from another source, in which case you might use it for a smaller personal plan.

New developments

As mentioned earlier, new and more sophisticated annuity-type products are being developed all the time. The latest – which requires a minimum fund of £250,000 – allows for a partial return of capital to heirs however late death occurs. It is vital to get professional advice before deciding on any of these new schemes.

The pensions choice: summary

Anyone coming up to retirement has clearly got some hard thinking to do. Of course, you can simply take what is offered by your pension company when you retire. You will automatically get a quotation for a fixed-interest annuity based on your age (and, if appropriate, that of your spouse) with and without the option of taking the tax-free cash, as well as information on escalating and index-linked annuities.

The annuity choice

Even if you decide that a conventional annuity is what you want, you should shop around to see if another provider offers a better deal. The answer is almost certain to be yes – and it could mean an improvement in your income of 5% or 10% every year for life. It is worth consulting a specialist financial adviser at this point because rates change constantly and it is a full-time job keeping up with them all. This advice will, in all likelihood, be free. Yes, the adviser will get commission from the pension company, but if you buy the annuity direct, you won't get a better deal – the company simply pockets the commission it would otherwise have paid. If your affairs are particularly complicated, you may be asked for a fee.

If you are retiring young, or have a much younger partner, you should seriously consider one of the alternatives to a fixed-interest annuity, such as the with-profits annuity, income withdrawal or perhaps staggered vesting. Which is right for you will depend on other factors, such as the overall state of your finances and, most important, your attitude to risk.

7

Insurance after retirement

Insurance is just as important after retirement as before. However, your needs may change as your age increases. This chapter covers:

- Life insurance
- Long-term care insurance
- Private medical insurance

Life insurance

Life insurance is vital to a young person with a growing family and a large mortgage. The family may be – for a time at least – entirely dependent on the income the main breadwinner earns and his or her premature death could make the surviving spouse and children not just penniless but homeless. But people at or approaching retirement are generally past that stage of life and it is time to reassess what, if any, life cover they need.

If you have been a member of a company pension scheme, you have probably been rather well insured in your later years. Most schemes pay a lump sum on "death in service" of up to four times annual salary in addition to a widow's or widower's pension. However, this lump sum cover ceases the day you retire.

So should you replace any of this, and if so, what type of policy should you choose? Life insurance can still be important if, for example:

- You have large debts such as a mortgage or car loan.
- You have financial responsibility for someone's university education.

◆ Your only significant asset (other than the pension) is your house, which you would like to leave to a son or daughter eventually, but fear they might not be able to pay the inheritance tax bill.

Whether it is needed in other cases depends on your circumstances. If nearly all your retirement income comes from your pension, remember that this is usually cut sharply if you die before your partner. Typically, pensions decline by a third at this point – this is normal practice with company final salary schemes. With money purchase schemes and personal pensions, the choice is yours: it is possible, as we have seen in earlier chapters, to opt for pensions that continue at half, two-thirds or all of the joint level. However, few choose the last option because this reduces the income considerably.

Many people feel that they would want to move to somewhere smaller and cheaper if their partner died. In this case, the lower pension income may be no great problem: they will have lower outgoings as well as a profit from trading down. However, few people would want to be forced to move immediately and it may take time to complete the sale and purchase. Because of this, it may be wise to have some money in reserve to meet these expenses. If you do not have this in ready cash, the answer may lie in some form of life insurance.

There may also come a time when you are no longer able to care for yourself and have to move into a residential home. One way of providing for this is to take out a long-term care insurance policy (see page 81) but premiums are expensive and couples may prefer that the ailing partner remains at home. But who would look after the survivor in such a case? Again, a straightforward life insurance policy that pays out a lump sum on the first death might be a better solution.

Whatever type of life insurance policy is chosen, premiums will be relatively expensive compared with those for younger ages. You may be tempted to go for the lowest available, but be warned: some policies can turn out to be false economies.

Life insurance: the choices

Let's assume you would like a lump sum of £25,000 after the first death. You can opt for a whole life policy, which guarantees to pay out on the first death whenever that might be, or a term assurance policy, which will pay out only if death occurs within an agreed term. At first sight, the latter may not seem suitable as there is always the chance you will both survive beyond that term – in which case you get nothing for your premiums. However, it is possible, at age 60 for example, to take out a term assurance policy for 30 or even 40 years.

Table 13, on page 78, gives some of the best rates currently available on different types of policy. Note that there are two sets of figures for whole life policies. The first, the lower figures, relate to policies written on a "maximum cover" basis and it is these which may prove a false economy. With these, the sum assured is guaranteed only if death occurs within ten years of the policy's inception. Thereafter, the premium rates and the level of cover are reviewed. If you want the premiums to stay the same, it could mean a big reduction in the sum assured.

Alternatively, if you want to keep the sum assured at the previous level, you may have to accept a significant increase in the premiums. This is probably the last thing you would want at the age of 70, particularly if your pension is not fully index-linked, as your disposable income after inflation will have declined in the intervening period. It would be more sensible to opt for the higher initial premiums charged by either the term assurance policy or the whole life policy written on a standard cover basis.

How to choose between the two? In one sense, term assurance is the least risky option, assuming, of course, that you do not live beyond the term chosen. This is because the sum assured is guaranteed, no matter what investment conditions are like. Under the whole life option, there is an underlying assumption that investment growth within the life fund will typically be 6% a year. If the fund fails to achieve this, premiums will have to rise to maintain cover, but not as much as they would under the maximum cover basis.

Table 13
The cost of life insurance

Monthly premiums for £25,000 sum assured

Type of policy	Man aged 60	Woman aged 60	Couple aged 60*
Term assurance			
25 years	£51	£30	£78
30 years	£54	£33	£85
40 years	£61	£39	£98
Whole life			
Maximum cover	£29	£19	£45
Standard cover	£62	£46	£82

*Sum assured payable on first death

Source: London & Country

Shopping around

It is definitely worth shopping around for the most competitive quotes for life insurance. For example, some companies charge more than £100 a month for the 25-year term assurance policy for a couple aged 60, compared with the £78 shown here. Similar discrepancies may be found for other ages or terms. You can use an insurance broker, or try shopping around yourself, either by phone or on the internet on www.lifesearch.co.uk. If you decide to do it yourself, make sure you read the small print. Life companies often use their own brand names for particular types of policy and it can take considerable scrutiny to work out what is being offered.

You can always try both routes. Brokers are not necessarily more expensive and may be especially useful if your case is a bit out of the ordinary or if you want to make sure the policy is appropriate for a particular purpose – for instance, if it is part of your inheritance tax planning strategy. The British Insurance Brokers' Association (020 7623 9043) will provide a list of local brokers or you can try *Yellow Pages*.

Terminal illness option

Most life companies will pay out the sum assured either on death or the diagnosis of a terminal illness, but this is a point that is worth checking. This option was not so common in the past, so if you have a policy that you took out some years ago, it may not be included.

Critical illness option

This is different from terminal illness. It is possible to buy a term assurance policy which will pay out not just in the event of death but on the diagnosis of a critical illness, such as certain forms of cancer, heart attacks, kidney failure and multiple sclerosis, or on permanent disability following an accident. These policies are significantly more expensive than straightforward term assurance, especially at older ages, and are probably not worth choosing once you are past retirement.

Medical examinations

If you are over 60 you should be prepared to undergo a medical examination before being accepted by a life company. If the results are poor, you might be turned down, but more commonly you will be accepted at higher premium rates (known as "loading" the premium).

There is an alternative: you can choose a special "no medical" policy. These are frequently advertised in the press. But their premiums are likely to be much higher. Unless you are in really poor health, it will always pay to choose a plan where a medical might be required. Its purpose is not necessarily to establish that you are super-fit, merely that you are in normal health for your age. As medical knowledge increases, the definition of normal has in some respects been widened and people who have suffered health problems in the past – particular forms of cancer, for example – might still be accepted for insurance, although it is likely to be at a higher premium.

Even if you have serious health problems, it may be worth making simultaneous applications, one for a no medical policy and one for a normal policy. Even if the second accepts you only at a loaded rate, it may still be cheaper than the no medical policy.

Joint life policies

The figures for the joint life policies shown in table 13 are for a "joint life, first death" policy, which means that the sum assured is paid out after the first of a couple dies. It is also possible to have a "joint life, last survivor" policy, which pays out only on the later death. If you want to provide funds for your partner, the first death option is the one you need. But the last survivor policies can provide your heirs with a cash sum, perhaps to help pay an inheritance tax bill (see chapter 16).

Life policies and tax

The sum assured paid on death is not in itself taxable. However, if the money is paid into your estate, it might give rise to an inheritance tax charge, so you should ensure the policy is written under a form of trust, which means the proceeds can be paid directly to the nominated beneficiaries. Although inheritance tax is not charged on assets being left by a husband to a wife (or vice versa), there is a further benefit in that sums assured under a policy written in trust can be paid out directly without waiting for a grant of probate.

Most life companies have a standard form of trust that is simple to use and will probably suit most people. But if your affairs are especially complex, or the off-the-shelf version does not suit for any reason, you may need expert advice on setting up a tailor-made trust. While it is possible to buy term assurance via the internet, it will not necessarily be set up under trust and trying to do so later will be more expensive.

Endowment policies

There is little point in starting an endowment after retirement – they are, after all, basically savings plans, and the financial emphasis post-retirement switches from saving to spending. However, you may have an endowment that is not due to mature until some years after retirement. You may be tempted to cash it in and save yourself the monthly outgoings, but this is likely to be bad value for money.

Ideally, you should continue making the payments until the policy matures. If your budget does not stretch to this, there are two alternatives:

- **Making the policy paid up** This means that no further premiums are payable and the policy will mature at its original date (for a lower sum).
- **Selling the policy on the second-hand endowment market** This is suitable only for with-profits policies, not the unit-linked variety. You are likely to get a better price for your policy by selling it than you will get by surrendering it to the life company. The Association of Policy Market Makers (see page 183) provides a list of

firms which deal in this market. The firms concerned will always establish what the surrender value would be and will sell it only if the price is higher than this – so you will not run the risk of losing out.

Long-term care insurance

Long-term care insurance is the name given to a variety of insurance policies which will pay out if you can no longer look after yourself and have to be cared for – either in your own home or in a residential or nursing home. The costs of such care can be enormous: £400 to £500 a week is by no means uncommon.

The state provides some help, but not that much, especially if you have considerable assets. People living in Wales and Scotland are better off than those living elsewhere, but anyone with even modest assets will find they have to meet most of the bills from their own resources.

Local authorities will pay care homes – who are expected to reduce their fees commensurately – the following sums for each resident:

- ◆ **England** Nursing care costs of £35 to £110 a week, depending on whether their nursing needs are assessed as moderate, middle range or high. There is no payment for personal care costs.
- ◆ **Scotland** From April 2002: nursing care costs of £65 a week plus personal care costs of £90 a week.
- ◆ **Wales** Nursing care costs of £100 a week. There is no payment for personal care costs.
- ◆ **Northern Ireland** Nothing.

There is no automatic provision that these figures will be raised in line with inflation.

These sums are not means-tested; in other words, they will be paid for every resident, regardless of their assets. The remainder of the bills must be paid by the individual if they have savings in excess of £18,500. You will be allowed to keep £16.05 a week for personal expenses, and if you have a pension and your spouse is still living at home, half the pension income is allowed to belong to them. Those with total savings of £11,500 to £18,500 must contribute some of the costs. Only those with less than £11,500 and no income to speak of will have everything paid by the state.

Your house will count as part of your assets, unless your spouse or a dependent relative under 16 is living there.

For the majority of people, therefore, it is likely that if they go into care, they will end up paying much of the cost themselves, and if they are on their own by the time this happens, their house may well have to be sold to pay the bill. So is insurance the answer? It might be, but it's hard to be categoric. Something like one in four people end up needing some form of residential care. One in four is high enough to make the premiums fairly expensive – but is not so high as to convince many people that it is worth taking out.

Perhaps the only answer is to be brutally clear sighted about the matter. Do you come from a family whose members live vigorously active lives until 90 and then drop dead? Or do they tend to go into a lengthy decline? The problem with this, of course, is that doctors are getting so much better at patching us up to last another few years that we cannot rely on the fact that our grandparents died smartly at the age of 80. The choice has to be an individual one: there is no right or wrong answer, but do be prepared at least to consider some form of insurance, along with the alternative of self-funding.

How long-term care insurance works

There are a number of types of policy. The first requires regular (usually monthly) premiums, which vary according to your age when the policy is taken out and the amount of benefit chosen (which is paid tax-free). Claims are payable when a policyholder becomes unable to carry out two or three (depending on the policy) of the following six "activities of daily living" – known as ADLs:

- General mobility (the ability to get out of a bed into a chair)
- Dressing
- Eating
- Bathing
- Using the lavatory
- Walking

Policies will also usually pay out if cognitive ability is impaired to the extent that it is unsafe for an individual to continue living at home. This category could include, for example, sufferers from Alzheimer's disease. Some policies will also pay for devices to help you stay in your own home.

Costs

Table 14 gives current premiums on a typical policy, which will pay £1,000 a month initially (index-linked thereafter) if the policyholder is unable to carry out two ADLs.

It is possible to buy cheaper policies. For example, if you were prepared for the benefit not to be index-linked and to be payable only once you were unable to carry out three ADLs, the premiums would be £56.04 monthly for the man aged 60 and £62.88 for the woman aged 60.

Table 14
The monthly cost of long-term care insurance

Age when policy bought	Man	Woman
60	£71.88	£90.60
65	£88.22	£113.64
70	£102.84	£148.38
75	£123.48	£192.12

Source: Norwich Union

You may be required to have a medical examination before being accepted. It may be possible to buy a policy for the first time at more than 75, but insurance companies tend not to publish premium rates for higher ages – the policies are underwritten individually.

Lump-sum plans

The second type of long-term care policy requires a substantial lump sum payment. The cash is then invested by the insurance company, which deducts money to pay the regular monthly premiums. If the insurance is needed, claims will be paid out; if not, the plan will have a cash value on death.

Immediate care plans

The third product offered by insurance companies is a special type of annuity, suitable for people who need to start paying for care immediately. The plan takes a lump sum and provides an annual income, which is paid directly to the nursing home. The income payments under this arrangement are wholly tax-free – which makes them better value than ordinary life annuities where an element of the income is taxable.

Where to find out more

This is an area where good independent advice is important. An organisation called Ifacare will provide the names of local independent financial advisers who have a special interest in advising on long-term care insurance. Call 01299 406040, log on to www.ifacare.co.uk or email info@ifacare.co.uk. At present, the sale of long-term care insurance is not regulated, but moves are afoot to force the Financial Services Authority to start doing so – in the meantime, proceed with care.

Another useful website is www.bettercaring.co.uk, which is run by the Stationery Office and provides a wealth of information on nursing homes and their costs – you can enter your postcode to find out about nursing homes in your area, for example.

Finally, Age Concern provides information via factsheets, telephone helplines and its website at www.ageconcern.org.uk.

Private medical insurance

Many people will have had private medical cover as a perk from their employer and may be reluctant to go back to relying on the National Health Service after retirement.

But insurance can be expensive and it is essential that you read the small print carefully. There are many schemes available, with premiums ranging from a few pounds a month to several hundred. As with most things in life, you get what you pay for. Some budget schemes, for example, will pay for private treatment only if the NHS has a waiting list in excess of a certain number of weeks. Further restrictions on the type of hospital allowed and the extent of cover can help cut the cost. Even with so-called comprehensive plans there may be a restriction on the amount that will be paid out for a single claim. One way of cutting the cost is to agree to meet the first part of any claim yourself – known as an excess. The higher the excess, the lower the premium will be.

Whatever type of cover you choose, you are unlikely to be insured for long-term illnesses or degenerative diseases associated with old age. Self-inflicted conditions arising from suicide attempts or drug or alcohol abuse may not be covered. If you have a pre-existing medical condition, this may either not be covered at all or may be subject to a moratorium, which means that you will not be able to claim for that problem for a certain time, say two years, after the policy begins.

It is essential when you apply for the insurance to tell the insurer everything that might be relevant. If you do not, and it emerges when you make a claim that you kept something back, your policy could be invalidated, leaving you to meet a hefty medical bill. The main areas of cover under a typical private medical policy are:

- Professional fees for consultants, specialist physicians, anaesthetists and surgeons.
- Hospital charges for accommodation and nursing, either in a private hospital or a private bed in an NHS hospital.
- Specialist treatments including physiotherapy, chemotherapy and radiology which can be taken as an in- or out-patient.
- The cost of drugs, tests, X-rays, dressings and treatments, out-patient treatments and home nursing.
- A cash benefit – typically £50 – paid for every night the policyholder receives treatment from the NHS. Some policies, known as hospital cash plans, provide only this sort of benefit.

The most common exclusions are:

- Fees payable to a general practitioner
- Treatments not recommended by a GP
- Dental treatments
- Cosmetic surgery
- Routine tests (such as for sight and hearing)
- Vaccinations
- Self-inflicted injuries

Table 15, on page 86, gives some examples of the cost of cover. Rates rise with age and are usually reviewed in line with medical inflation, which means they are likely to rise at least once a year. If the past is anything to go by, rises will be fairly steep: medical inflation has been running at 8% to 12% for the past few years.

Table 15
The cost of private medical insurance

Monthly premiums for a couple*

	Age 65	Age 75
Local hospitals, no excess	£243.41	£354.19
Local hospitals, £100 excess	£233.67	£347.11
Local hospitals, £2,000 excess	£143.62	£212.52
National hospitals, no excess	£275.06	£400.24
National hospitals, £100 excess	£264.05	£392.24
National hospitals, £2,000 excess	£162.29	£240.14

*Premium rates relate to a couple living in Oxford, both non-smokers

Source: Bupa

Some retired people will decide they have better uses for their income than paying regular premiums for private medical insurance. They may decide that if, at some stage, they do need hospital treatment, they will pay out of capital for private treatment – it's an entirely personal decision.

8
Investing in retirement – finding advice

Retirement is the time when you stop being a money-making machine in your own right and must look to your pensions and savings to produce that income for you. With the lump sum available from many pension plans, and perhaps the proceeds of various endowment policies, many people will be faced with what seems like an enormous amount of cash, which must be invested to produce the income required. So it is likely that, maybe for the first time in your life, you will need expert financial advice. This chapter will tell you about:

◆ The different types of financial adviser
◆ How to pay for advice: commission or fees
◆ How to find an adviser
◆ How to judge one
◆ How to complain if things go wrong

Of course, you can avoid all this and just put the cash on deposit at a local building society, but it is unlikely to be the best answer. There is nothing to stop you undertaking your own research and constructing your own investment portfolio, but many people do not have sufficient knowledge of – or interest in – investment to make their own decisions. Even those who are experts in the field may prefer to let someone else take the strain – I have known of at least one investment director of a big City firm who believes it is better to let someone else manage his money as he has neither the time nor the inclination to do it himself.

One of the most common questions asked by readers of *The Sunday Times* is: "Where can I find a good financial adviser I can trust?" Unless you are an expert yourself, taking advice inevitably means taking things on trust, but recent financial scandals, such as the mis-selling of personal pensions and mortgage endowments, have undoubtedly made people wary of financial salespeople. After all, they are, in most cases, rewarded for their efforts by receiving commission on products sold, which hardly seems conducive to the provision of unbiased advice.

Types of adviser

Financial advisers and salespeople are currently divided into two categories. The first are independent and must look at the whole range of products or services available in the marketplace to establish the most appropriate ones for their clients' needs. The second are employees or "appointed representatives" of particular companies – generally life assurers – who are allowed only to sell or advise on the products of their own company. They cannot even comment on the suitability of anyone else's product. They are often called tied agents. In legal terms, the independent adviser is the agent of his client, whereas the employee or representative is an agent of his company.

Under the 1986 Financial Services Act, all financial companies and individuals giving advice are regulated by the Financial Services Authority (FSA). Both types of adviser must obey a great many rules and regulations, and individuals must have passed a number of exams before they are allowed to give advice to the public. They are bound to provide advice that is appropriate to their clients' needs, bearing mind their circumstances, financial aims and attitude to risk.

The existence of these rules does not, of course, mean they are always followed. The key thing is that if they are not, individuals are entitled to complain and may receive compensation. The FSA inspects firms regularly and if one is found to have broken the rules, it may impose a fine or, in the last resort, withdraw authorisation from that company or from individuals working for it, making it illegal for them to continue offering advice.

Tied versus independent

Of the two general types of adviser, the independent ones should – all other things being equal – be a better choice, simply because they have a wider range of investments and products to choose from. Some organisations, such as high street banks, may run both types of business. However, unless you specifically request independent advice, you are likely to be directed towards the bank's tied service, where employees can advise only on the bank's own investment and insurance products.

Stockbrokers

If you want advice mainly on the handling of an investment portfolio, a private client stockbroker might be the right choice. Stockbrokers, like more general financial advisers, are regulated by the Financial Services Authority and must pass professional exams and obey the regulations. Those who cater for private clients can be loosely divided into three categories:

- Execution-only – in other words, they merely carry out buy and sell orders without providing any advice.
- Those prepared to look after "small" clients – with upwards of maybe £50,000 to invest – and who would, in the main, use pooled investments such as unit and investment trusts.
- Those at the top end who prefer their clients to have a minimum of perhaps £250,000 to £1m to invest. Some merchant banks are also contenders for this type of business.

Some brokers offer only "discretionary management", which means they take complete responsibility for making investment decisions on the client's behalf, without prior consultation (though they are, of course, obliged to inform their clients of what they have done). Non-discretionary management means that brokers will provide advice but not initiate any action unless specifically requested to do so by their client. Generally speaking, discretionary management is the more practical and less costly option for both parties.

Other sources of advice

While most financial advisers are regulated by the Financial Services Authority, some firms of accountants and solicitors may also offer financial advice and, depending on whether it is a small or large part of their overall business, they may be regulated by their own professional body, such as the Institute of Chartered Accountants or the Law Society.

Actuaries usually work for life insurance companies, but there are some firms of independent consultants who will work for members of the public on a fee-paying basis. You might need one in a specialist area such as pension transfers.

Paying for advice

All advice costs money, but some of these costs are more hidden than others. Life company employees usually get a basic salary but they will also be rewarded by commission on products sold. Independent advisers can be paid either by commission or directly by fees. Few independent firms charge fees only – many will offer you the choice of whether to pay by commission or a fee. Where a fee-charging adviser recommends a commission-paying product, the commission will either be refunded to you or invested in the product. Stockbrokers who provide advice can follow either route; some give clients the choice of fees or commission.

If you have considerable sums to invest, it may be preferable to opt for a fee charging adviser rather than one who takes commission only. Not only will you feel happier with this but it could save you money. Fees are charged by the hour, so you can help yourself by being well prepared for meetings, with clear details of your existing assets and having given some thought to your future requirements.

Even if you decide on the fee-based route, it may be better if you allow your adviser to take his fees out of the commission. This is because it is more tax efficient: you do not pay Vat on commission but you do on fees.

Commission disclosure

All financial companies have to disclose the amount of commission they pay on products to everyone who buys them, along with full details of the charges being deducted. That means, mostly, unit trusts and Isas, pensions, life assurance policies and bonds.

Although it is good that the amount of commission has to be disclosed, it is not always of great practical use to investors. Knowing that your adviser is getting £100 for the product he has recommended to you, does not get you very far. Would a similar product pay more or less? Are you getting a bargain or paying through the nose? Is it fair payment for the time the adviser has spent on your case? None of these questions is answered by the figure itself.

Any type of cost may be off-putting to people who, hitherto, have dealt only with building societies for their investment needs, because there appears to be no charge for a savings account. Of course, if one compares the mortgage rate charged to borrowers with the interest rate paid to savers, it becomes evident that the true cost lies in the gap between the two.

Commission versus charges

It is easy to concentrate solely on the amount of commission payable on a particular product, but this is a mistake. What is of real importance is the overall charges levied on the investment. These, too, must be disclosed to buyers, although, again, it may be difficult to judge whether something is expensive or cheap unless you know what similar products charge. In the chapters that follow, the impact of charges will be made clear in relation to particular products.

One point you should be aware of is that buying direct from a company will not usually save you money. The company merely keeps the commission it would otherwise have paid to the adviser.

How to find an independent adviser

The organisation IFA Promotion will provide the names of three independent advisers near your home or office. Call 0800 085 3250 with details of your postcode. You will be sent a voucher for a free initial consultation. You can ask for an adviser who specialises in a particular area and IFAP runs checks that any adviser offering such a specialisation has taken the appropriate exams. You can also specify if you want an adviser who charges fees as opposed to taking commission. The list is not exhaustive as it represents only those who subscribe to IFAP, but it covers about three-quarters of the total.

The Money Management Register of Fee-based Advisers will provide a list of six names and addresses, again on the basis of proximity to your home or office, all of whom charge fees. The firms are vetted regularly to ensure they are fully authorised. You can specify an adviser with a particular area of expertise, for example, ethical investment or pensions, and the first half hour of consultation is free. Telephone 0870 013 1925 or write to Freepost 22 (SW1 565), London W1E 1BR. You can also find details of advisers at www.ukifadirectory.co.uk.

The Stock Exchange runs a public information line on 020 7797 1372, which will send out stockbrokers' names and addresses. The Association of Private Client Investment Managers and Stockbrokers (APCIMS) provides a list of its 200 members and the services they offer. Write to APCIMS, 112 Middlesex Street, London E1 7HY; telephone 020 7247 7080, or see its website, www.apcims.co.uk.

Choosing an adviser

There is no magic route to finding the perfect adviser. It helps if you know a bit about the issues yourself, largely because that will give you more confidence to ask questions on matters that have not been made clear and to judge the value of the answers given. Never be afraid to ask questions. If you have not understood something the first time, that is a failure on the part of the adviser to explain it properly.

You must also be prepared for some in-depth grilling on the state of your financial affairs and your aims and attitudes. Not only is this required by law under the Financial Services Act, but no decent adviser could expect to give proper advice without knowing your full background.

It is only sensible to be realistic in your choice of an adviser, and to expect him or her to be realistic with you. If your investment portfolio totals £10,000 it is a waste of your adviser's time (and your money) to insist on management by some gold-plated merchant bank.

In the end, don't be afraid of trusting your own instincts. You should be wary of an adviser who tells you he is always right or that he can make you rich overnight. Anyone who claims this is a fool or a fraud – possibly both. If, after a meeting with an adviser, you do not like him, try someone else – it's as simple as that.

If things go wrong

If things go badly wrong, don't be afraid to complain. You should take your complaint first to the company concerned, but if it refuses to listen or fails to offer a satisfactory solution, you should go to the Financial Ombudsman Service (FOS) or, if it concerns a company pension matter, to the pensions ombudsman at the Office for the Pensions Advisory Service (See page 178).

The ombudsman's service is free for investors, but it will consider your complaint only if you have first given the company a chance to put matters right and it has failed to do so. There are also a series of time limits within which you can approach the ombudsman. The main one is within six months after you have received the final letter from the company concerned turning your complaint down. It should also be within six years of the problem happening, or within three years of your becoming aware of it, if that is later. The FOS has a free leaflet guiding people on how to make a complaint: *Your Complaint and the Ombudsman*, which is available from 0845 080 1800.

The ombudsman is strictly impartial so do not expect it will automatically be on your side. If it does decide a dispute in your favour, however, it can award compensation.

Where it decides a product has been wrongly sold to you, the principle by which it awards compensation is to put you back in the position you would have been in had you not bought it. Very occasionally, it may also order a further payment for distress and serious inconvenience.

However, it will not, for example, order an adviser to pay back money simply because an investment he recommended went down in value. As long as he explained the risks of stock market investment to you and it was appropriate to your circumstances at the time of the investment, you have no valid reason for a complaint.

9

Planning your post-retirement portfolio

Investment planning is usually an exercise in achieving the best possible compromise between conflicting aims. All investors would like to put their money in an investment which provides a high – and rising – income, good capital growth, no risk and is tax-free. If only!

Of course, there is no such thing. Some investments will give a decent income but little or no prospect of growth; others might provide the prospect of growth but with risk attached. This chapter covers:

- The importance of inflation
- The first steps to planning a portfolio
- The layered approach
- Different asset classes

Stocktaking for inflation

This might seem a quaintly old-fashioned exercise – after all, inflation is dead and buried, isn't it? The only possible answer is – maybe, but maybe not. Certainly, in the last few years, we have seen the rate of inflation plummet, from double figures in the late 1980s to about 2% today. But if you are retiring in your early 60s, you could be looking at 20, 25 or even 30 years to come during which your savings must earn their keep – and that is plenty of time for even a seemingly well-entrenched economic trend to be turned on its head.

In any case, as table 16 shows, even at today's low rates, inflation will eat away at the purchasing power of your money. At an annual rate of 2%, the £100 in your pocket at age 60 will buy only £82.03 worth of goods by the time you reach 70 and just £60.95 worth once you reach 85.

Table 16
Real value of £100 after inflation at the following rates

Years	2%	3%	4%
1	£98.04	£97.08	£96.15
5	£90.57	£86.26	£82.29
10	£82.03	£74.41	£67.56
15	£74.30	£64.19	£55.53
20	£67.30	£55.36	£45.64
25	£60.95	£47.76	£37.51

Even if your income is fully linked to the retail price index, the chances are you will feel poorer as the years go by, because the income of most people – in other words, people still in employment – will be rising faster than price inflation. Table 17 compares price and earnings inflation over the last few years.

Table 17
Price and earnings inflation

Year (Jan)	Price inflation	Earnings inflation
1995	3.3%	3.6%
1996	2.9%	2.9%
1997	2.8%	4.3%
1998	3.3%	4.8%
1999	2.4%	4.3%
2000	2.0%	6.1%
2001	2.7%	4.1%

First step to planning

As a first step to planning your post-retirement portfolio, you need to take an inventory of your assets, your income and your liabilities. Your running liabilities – such as rates, insurance, utility bills and so forth – will, on the whole, increase in line with inflation. But what about your income?

Start with your pensions. To what extent, if any, will these increase to match inflation? It all depends. State pensions (the basic state pension plus Serps) will increase in line with inflation. If you have a company pension from a good final salary scheme, the likelihood is that this, too, will increase in line with inflation, although it may not be guaranteed to do so. If yours is a public sector pension from your work as a civil servant or teacher, for example, the pension is guaranteed to be index-linked. But if you are relying on a personal pension or one from a company money purchase scheme, you may have chosen a pension which is level for the rest of your life, with no provision for any increases.

If you are married, you should bear in mind that total pension income may well be cut after the first death. Company pension schemes generally provide a widow's or widower's pension of half or two-thirds the main pension. Those with personal pensions can opt for a plan which continues to pay the full pension after the planholder's death, but this option is significantly more expensive and few people choose it.

However prudently you have saved for your pension, it is likely that you will be facing a big drop in income on retirement.

It's not all bad news, however. By the time you retire, you should, with luck, have paid off your mortgage and seen your children through university. With even more luck, you will have seen them settled in careers and buying their own homes. You might even feel positively rich compared to your cash-strapped middle years.

Nevertheless, with a long retirement ahead, you will need to invest wisely to ensure that at least some of your income is inflation-proofed. If all your pension income is index-linked, there is less need to worry. But if the majority of it is not, you need to put a higher proportion of your free assets into investments where the income is capable of growing over time.

Second step: taking the layered approach

It is a basic maxim of financial planning that money should be spread among different types of investment, with different degrees of risk. There are three basic building blocks, or asset classes:
- Cash – not the folding stuff itself, of course, but bank deposit accounts and similar products
- Fixed-interest securities – government and corporate bonds
- Equities (company shares)

Table 18 is a thumbnail sketch, highlighting the main differences between the three.

Table 18
Asset classes

	Capital security	Income yield	Growth potential: income	Growth potential: capital
Cash Building society and bank deposit accounts, cash Isas, Tessas, National Savings etc	High	High	None	None
Fixed interest Government securities (gilts), corporate bonds, Pibs etc	Medium	Medium	None (except index-linked gilts)	None
Equities Company shares and products that invest in them – eg unit trusts investment trusts, equity Isas, life insurance bonds etc	Low	Low	High	High

Only investments within the cash class offer 100% capital security and a reasonable income from the start. Only equities and index-linked gilts provide the prospect of a growing income together with capital growth. On the minus side for equities is the fact that their starting yield is low and for all their "potential" there is, of course, risk: both the capital and the income they provide may fall.

Looking back, equities have performed tremendously and have handsomely outpaced any other form of investment. Figure 1 shows how the three main classes – equities, fixed-interest securities and cash (represented by treasury bills) have performed over the long term, adjusted for inflation.

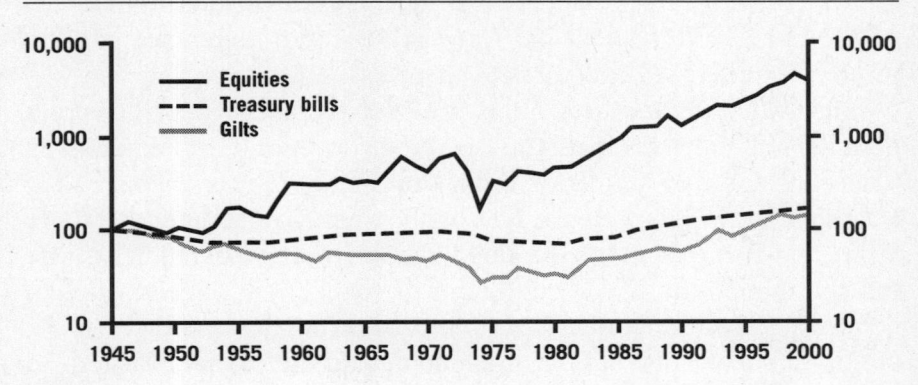

Figure 1
Equity investment, gross income reinvested, in real terms after allowing for inflation.

Source: Barclays Capital

You may be tempted to conclude from this that investment is easy – all you have to do is pile all your money into equities and sit back and watch it grow. Until the end of the last century, almost all the evidence would have seemed to back you up. But the last couple of years have been distinctly rocky for equity investments. Even if you succeeded in avoiding "dotcom" mania, your stock market investments will have suffered as markets worldwide have taken a tumble, and many people have learned, for perhaps the first time, that – as the advertisements say – "the value of your investments may go down as well as up".

There is only one answer to this. Boring as it may seem, it is to have a spread of risk: to split your money between the three asset classes, so if things go wrong on the stock market, you will be protected to at least some extent.

How much should you have in each class? That is a "how long is a piece of string" question. Everyone needs the first layer of capital secure investments – cash deposits – for emergencies, for capital expenditure you know will be coming up, such as replacing your car, and as basic security. This layer will also produce a decent, regular income.

If you have capital surplus to these needs, you can afford to branch out into the other asset classes, but this depends on you. Except for index-linked gilts, or gilts you are determined to hold until maturity, once you leave the haven of cash, you say goodbye to capital security. Can you live with the prospect of seeing the value of your investments fall? It may be a temporary fall, but given that we cannot see into the future, it may be hard to convince ourselves of this.

If investing in equities is going to give you sleepless nights, then don't do it – it's as simple as that. The last thing you want in retirement is to have constant money worries. But if you can, try to spread your risk at least a bit: even if you hate the idea of uncertainty, remember that there is no getting away from it in life. Building society accounts might feel safe but the income they pay can be cut dramatically if interest rates in general fall. We never know when or if inflation might make a comeback, cutting the real value of both the income and the capital invested. So even if you are reluctant to expose a large part of your portfolio to the risk of the stock market, you could still consider putting 10% or 20% of your assets into equities.

Chapter 13 provides examples of model portfolios for people with different circumstances. They are not a blueprint for successful investment – the financial advisers who have prepared them are no more infallible than the rest of us. But you will see that the theme of them all is a spread of risk. Any decent adviser would advocate the same.

Finally, before we look at these asset classes in detail, a word of warning. Financial companies are well aware that investors, in general, dislike risk. Because, naturally enough, they want to sell their products, they do their best to design products which limit risk – fair enough – but they also present them in a way which minimises the amount of risk actually involved. This is not always a matter of being misleading – you can be sure any mainstream product will have passed the strict regulatory tests on what can and cannot be said – but it can be a matter of nuance, of emphasis.

Remember the old investment adage: if something seems too good to be true, it probably is. If a particular investment looks terrific, make yourself read the whole brochure again. You'll probably spot the drawback second time round. It may not stop you investing – but at least you'll know where you are.

10

Low-risk investments

These are the appropriate home for your emergency money and for at least the first chunk of your investment portfolio. How much you put away here depends partly on your attitude to risk and partly on the size of your overall assets. However brave you are, if your investments total, say, £10,000, you'll probably want to keep most, possibly all, of your money here. This chapter covers:

◆ Your tax position
◆ The age allowance trap
◆ Variable and fixed-rate investments
◆ Other capital secure investments
◆ Credit risk

Check your tax position

The three main providers of these products are banks, building societies and National Savings. Because they pay interest, which is for the most part taxable, it's worth making use of all the tax breaks you can get.

If you are not personally liable to tax, make sure you are getting your interest gross. Some of the National Savings products pay it this way. Bank and building society accounts deduct basic rate tax at 20%, but if you are not liable, you can get the interest paid gross by filling out form R85, available from your bank or building society. Alternatively, you can claim back the tax via your tax return, but this is a needlessly convoluted way of doing things. Higher rate taxpayers must declare the interest on their return and pay an extra 20%.

Married couples should look at their overall tax position. If one partner has a company pension, this counts and is taxed as that person's income. If the wife, for instance, has no pension income of her own, she should hold sufficient assets in cash deposits to make full use of her personal allowance. Remember, this is not a fixed sum: as interest rates have come down, the amount of capital in the wife's name can be increased before she will be liable to pay any tax, as the following example shows.

Paul Brown retired two years ago at age 65 with a company pension of £20,000. He retired with a tax-free lump sum of £60,000 and at the same time collected the proceeds of two maturing endowment policies totalling £30,000. His wife Jane, who was 63 at the time, had no pension or other income of her own. The couple did some sums and decided that, with interest running at 7% on the best-paying accounts, they should transfer £60,000 into her name so she could pick up the annual income, totalling £4,200, tax-free – as this was below her tax-free personal allowance of £4,355.

Two years later, they do the sums again: Jane has now reached 65, which means she qualifies for the higher, age-related personal allowance of £5,990 in the tax year 2001-02. At the same time, interest rates have fallen to 5%. They realise they could transfer the remaining £30,000 into her name as well and the total income that it now produces, £4,500, would be well below her personal allowance.

If you are fortunate enough to have such a large pension on retirement that you are liable to higher rate tax, this shifting of capital is still worthwhile if your partner pays tax at a lower rate.

If you prefer to keep joint accounts at your bank or building society, incidentally, the Inland Revenue will assume that the money is split 50:50 between you, but you can elect to have it treated differently – perhaps 60:40 or 70:30. The rule is that this must reflect the reality of the situation; you cannot simply state the account belongs 90% to your (non-taxpaying) spouse if in reality you dictate wholly how it is used. Quite how the Revenue would check up on this, I have no idea – but, in theory, it could try.

The age allowance trap

Once you are over 65, you are entitled to a higher personal allowance. In the 2001-02 tax year, this is £5,990, compared to £4,535 for the under 65s. But you get to keep it only if your income is below a certain level – £17,600 in the 2001-02 tax year. Once your income exceeds this, the extra amount is withdrawn at the rate of £1 for every £2 of extra income you receive. Once your personal allowance is back to the ordinary, under-65 level, it sticks there – you cannot lose any more.

If your income is well above the band at which the trap operates, there is nothing much you can do about it. But if you are stuck in the middle, it is worth considering investments which pay interest tax-free – that means cash Isas and various National Savings products such as the fixed-interest and index-linked certificates (see below for more details).

But how can you check whether the latest issue of five-year, fixed-rate National Savings certificates, for instance, which pay 3.5% tax-free, is worth more or less to you in the hand than a taxable building society account paying 5%, where the interest lands you straight in the age allowance trap?

What you need to do is to gross up the National Savings tax-free rate by 33%: in other words, divide 3.5 by 0.67. In this case, 3.5% is equivalent to a gross rate of 5.22% – so, in fact, you will be better off after tax with the National Savings certificate.

Variable rate investments

For a proper spread of risk, you should have some money in variable rate accounts and some in fixed-rate deposits. Banks and building societies are the main providers of variable rate accounts, though National Savings may also be a contender.

It always pays to check periodically that you are getting the best rates available. If you have access to the internet, www.moneyfacts.co.uk is a good place to check rates. Most of the weekend papers run tables of "best buy" savings accounts, with a number of options listed depending on notice period, minimum investment and so on. Moneyfacts also publishes a monthly magazine which provides details of all rates payable on savings accounts.

These days, the best-paying accounts are almost invariably internet-based, telephone or postal accounts. Branch-based accounts, for the most part, pay far less. So, unless you have a sentimental attachment to your building society branch, there is little point in keeping money there.

Are you a rate tart?

Financial services companies have a name for those of us who move our accounts regularly to ensure we are getting the best rates available: they call us "rate tarts". As you might gather, they are not too keen on us – but they have brought it on their own heads thanks to their practice of launching new, attractive accounts and letting older accounts become gradually less competitive. Everyone is beginning to realise that this is rather futile and the practice seems to be a little less prevalent than it was. For branch-based accounts, banks and building societies must publicise their new rates within the branches within three days of a rate change. If you have a postal or internet account, under the Banking Code, you must be notified personally within 30 days.

Is there any point in carpetbagging?

Carpetbagging was a favourite pastime of investors a few years ago – opening a large number of small accounts with a variety of mutual building societies in the hope that they would go public and bring their investors a windfall. This activity has tailed off in recent years, partly because there are fewer mutuals and partly because those that remain have sought to protect themselves by bringing in rules to ensure that new members donate any windfall to charity. Some societies – such as the Nationwide – have no time limit on this requirement, but most of the others which have brought in such a measure decree that new members will be entitled to keep any windfall only once they have been with the society for five or ten years.

In the current economic climate, there is less pressure on societies to go public than there was, and there seems little point in carpetbagging these days – especially if it means forgoing a better interest rate elsewhere.

Cash Isas and Tessas

It makes sense to have as much as possible of your interest-bearing deposits in a tax-free home. This means either an Isa – an individual savings account – or a Tessa – a tax-exempt special savings account. Tessas were five-year term accounts on sale until April 1999. Once your

Low-risk investments

Tessa completes its term you can transfer the capital (but not the interest) into a special Tessa-only Isa. The maximum you can transfer is £9,000. Once within the Isa regime, money can be withdrawn at any time without losing the tax-free status, but once withdrawn, you cannot top it up again. However, you can transfer to another provider if you find a better rate elsewhere.

The individual savings account was brought in as a replacement for both Tessas and Peps (personal equity plans). Investors can save up to £7,000 a year in an Isa, but only a portion of this can go into a cash Isa. The rules are complicated. There are two options:

Mini Isas (using three separate providers)	or	Maxi Isas (using one provider)
£3,000 into a cash Isa £1,000 into an insurance Isa £3,000 into an equity Isa		£7,000 in total, with no more than £3,000 in cash, £1,000 in insurance and £7,000 in equities/corporate bonds

Each year, you must choose either the mini route or the maxi route – you cannot have one of each in the same tax year. If you do, the later one will be invalidated, even if you have invested less than £7,000 in total during that year.

The maxi Isa is more flexible in theory, because you could decide, for example, to invest £3,000 in cash and £4,000 in equities. But there is a practical problem. Very few of the managers which offer maxi Isas include all three elements. Indeed, most of the big names in equity investment offer Isas that invest only in equities. So if you want to put money into a cash Isa, you will be more or less forced to go down the mini route.

If you're not interested in investing in equities, the message is clear: you should invest the maximum in a cash Isa each year. As well as being tax-free, most of the leading providers treat their cash Isas as a flagship account, paying top rates of interest. Most cash Isas allow penalty-free withdrawals, but don't take the money out if you can help it. While the bank or building society may not impose a penalty, once withdrawn, you cannot reinvest money into the Isa within the same tax year.

National Savings income bonds

These pay variable interest and three months' notice is required for withdrawals. The rate tends to be reasonably competitive with bank and building society accounts but is rarely as good as the best. For example, at time of writing, deposits of less than £25,000 attracted 4.1% interest and £25,000-plus, 4.35%, while the top-paying bank accounts still paid just over 5%. Interest is automatically paid gross, but it is taxable.

Fixed-rate investments

Cash Isas

A few Isa providers offer a fixed rate. Generally speaking, fixed rates will be slightly lower than variable ones (especially if the general consensus is that interest rates are on a downward trend).

National Savings certificates: fixed and indexed

Rates on these certificates are both fixed and tax-free, making them especially useful for higher rate taxpayers or for people caught in the age allowance trap (see above). They are not at all attractive for anyone not liable to tax.

Both types offer a choice of two and five-year terms. The fixed-rate certificates pay a rate averaged over the term, while index-linked certificates pay a fixed supplement in addition to inflation during the term. While in each case you can withdraw capital before the end of the term, you may lose out on interest – withdrawals in the first year, for example, can mean no interest is paid at all.

If investors do not elect to cash in their holding at the end of the term, they are automatically rolled over into the appropriate current issue – so five-year, fixed-rate holders get the new five-year, fixed-rate certificate, two-year, index-linked holders the new two-year, index-linked certificate. In the case of a rolled-over investment, investors can cash in within the first year and receive pro-rata interest, whereas with a new investment, no interest is payable if it is cashed in during the first year.

National Savings pensioners' bonds

These are available only to those over 60. They pay a fixed, taxable rate for one, two or five years, with income paid gross and monthly. The minimum investment is £500 and the maximum £1m.

Where to find National Savings rates

To find out the current National Savings rates, see the website, www.nationalsavings.co.uk, or phone the customer enquiry line on 0845 964 5000 (open 8am to 8pm Monday to Friday, 9am to 1pm Saturday), see the leaflets which should be available in all post offices, or you can check on BBC2 Ceefax (page 257).

Guaranteed income bonds

These bonds are issued by life companies and pay a fixed rate of interest for their term, which may be anything from one to five years. Income is usually paid out once a year, net of basic rate tax which cannot be reclaimed. Higher rate taxpayers must pay extra, although the way the bonds are structured usually means that the additional amount payable is relatively low. It is a good idea to check what happens if the bondholder dies during the year, between income payments – some bonds pay out interest pro rata, while others pay no interest at all for that year. Details of current offers can usually be found in the weekend press.

Gilts held to maturity

Government securities, known as gilts pay a fixed rate of interest. Gilts are negotiable securities, which means you do not have to buy them at the time they were issued. Instead, you can buy them from another holder via the Stock Exchange. Unless the gilts are bought at issue, when the price is fixed, purchasers must pay the going rate, which is dictated by the general level of interest rates. Likewise, if you want to sell them before they reach maturity, the price you get is not guaranteed and will depend on interest rates at that time. So the only way that gilts can provide total security for your capital is if you to hold them until maturity.

For example, at the time of writing, it cost £119.51 to buy £100 nominal of Treasury 8½% 2007, because interest rates have moved down since the stock was issued back in 1986. At this price, the running yield on the stock – the amount of income you will get each year until it matures – is 7.11%. However, because the stock will be redeemed for £100, there is a guaranteed capital loss waiting for you. Building this loss into the calculation produces the redemption yield, which works out at 4.57%.

Stockbrokers crunch these numbers on a daily basis as prices move. You can also find interest and redemption yields quoted in papers such as the *Financial Times*.

You can either buy through a stockbroker or, if you are not concerned about the exact timing of the purchase, via the Bank of England. A booklet on buying gilts in this way is available from the Bank by calling 0800 818614. You can also find a guide to buying gilts on the website of the Debt Management Office, www.dmo.gov.uk, under publications.

Index-linked gilts

If you want a rock-solid investment, this is it. Along with National Savings index-linked certificates, it is the only thing that provides a guaranteed real return. The interest will rise in line with the retail price index, as will the capital value, so long as investors hold on to their gilts until redemption. The drawback with index-linked gilts is that the initial level of income is very low, around 2% gross.

Having said they are rock-solid, one question springs to mind, now that inflation is so low: what would happen if we moved to a situation of deflation? You would still get back, on maturity, the real value of the capital invested at issue, but this could be less than the original monetary value, if deflation were really to take off.

Interest on gilts is usually paid gross, though you can opt for it to be paid net of basic rate tax.

Other capital secure investments

Guaranteed equity bonds

This is the general name given to a variety of investment products, all of which use financial futures or options of some type to provide a combination of guaranteed capital with some exposure to possible future growth in the stock market. The underlying structure of these bonds can be very complex and – for the financial layman – extremely difficult to understand. They are, in effect, a half-way house for investors who would like to benefit from stock market growth but are unwilling to risk the security of their capital, and they have proved very popular with investors.

Nevertheless, there is a price to be paid for the guarantee. A typical product, currently available, lasts for a five-year term and pays 75% of the average increase in four stock market indices – the FTSE-100, the Eurostoxx 50, the S&P 500 and the Swiss Market index. If markets fall during this period, investors are guaranteed their capital back in full.

Low-risk investments

This might sound wonderful, like having your cake and eating it, but there are a number of disadvantages. The first is that the investment earns no interest or income during the term. The second is that if the markets concerned were to rise between the start and end date, but fall back to where they were when the bond started, investors would not be able to profit by selling early. Furthermore, most bonds use a combination of market indices – many, for example, use one of the Japanese indices – and it becomes almost impossible to gauge the risk you are taking. Finally, most have a cap on the total gain, so if markets do take off, you would not benefit fully from the rise.

The bonds can have different structures as regards tax, which have differing implications for basic and higher rate taxpayers.

These bonds are generally limited issues and terms can change overnight. If you are attracted by this kind of investment, it is sensible to get independent advice before choosing which one to buy.

Credit risk

To describe any investment as risk-free is perhaps erroneous, in that there is always the possibility (however remote) that the organisation which holds your money will go bust. Investors should at least be aware of the limits of the various compensation schemes.

- **National Savings products** Guaranteed by the government. No other guarantee, or compensation scheme, is necessary – or possible.
- **Bank and building society deposits** 100% of the first £2,000 plus 90% of the next £33,000 per individual can be recovered under the Financial Services Compensation Scheme.
- **Life insurance products** 90% of the value of the policy can be recovered.
- **Other products** The Financial Services Compensation Scheme provides protection for investors where a financial company has had a complaint upheld against it by the regulator or by the Financial Services Ombudsman and where an award has been made to the investor. If the firm is unable to pay and goes into liquidation, the scheme can provide maximum compensation per individual of £48,000, representing 100% of the first £30,000 plus 90% of the next £20,000.

There is no compensation for losses incurred through normal market risk except where it can be proved that the individual was wrongly advised to buy particular products bearing in mind their aims, circumstances and attitudes at the time of purchase. The fact that something turns out to be a poor investment is not proof that advice to invest in it was wrong.

Warning: don't believe every % sign you see

There are many other products catering for the income-seeking investor which are often advertised with a mouth-watering figure before that % sign. If that figure is much above the current going rate from a bank or building society, you can be 100% sure that there is a catch. It means that the capital is not secure.

The product may be a corporate bond fund, where investors run the risk that some of the underlying investments will prove worthless if the companies issuing those bonds go bust, and others may fall in price if the market perceives the default risk to be high. Or it may be a stock market-linked high income bond, where the level of income is guaranteed for the term, but the return of capital depends on the performance of one or more market indices. Or it could be a with-profits bond fund, where the first year's bonus level may be guaranteed but subsequent bonuses depend on the performance of the (largely equity-based) with-profits fund.

We look at these products in more detail in the next chapter. Some or all of them may well have their place in a diversified portfolio, but it is vital to realise that they are not risk-free.

11
Medium-risk investments

The investments which occupy the next step up the risk ladder are a mixed bunch. They include gilts that are not held to maturity, corporate bond funds and with-profits bonds. There is no absolute guarantee with any of these investments that capital will be returned intact, but they are, by and large, not as risky as equity investments, and the returns over the years will be likely to fall somewhere between no-risk and high-risk investments. This chapter covers:

◆ Gilts
◆ Corporate bonds
◆ Permanent interest-bearing shares (Pibs)
◆ With-profits bonds
◆ High income bonds

Gilts

In the last chapter we saw that gilts can provide predictable returns only if they are held until maturity. Should you sell before that date, the proceeds will reflect the interest rate at the time you sell. If interest rates have risen since you bought, you will make a loss; if they have fallen, you will make a profit. Few private investors buy and sell gilts on a regular basis, though such holdings may well be a part of an actively managed portfolio run by a stockbroker. Alternatively, you can buy a unit trust specialising in gilts.

Income-seeking investors should remember that gilts will rise in value only if interest rates have fallen – so, while you might be able to realise a profit, you would not be able to reinvest elsewhere to provide the same level of income.

Interest from gilts is usually paid gross but it is taxable. You can opt for it to be paid net of basic rate tax. Any capital gains you make from selling gilts are tax-free, but any losses you make cannot be set against gains made elsewhere to reduce your capital gains tax liability. Gilt funds are not eligible for inclusion in an Isa.

Corporate bonds

What they are

When companies need money, they have three main ways to raise it: they can issue new share capital, borrow from the bank or issue a bond, a longer-term fixed-interest security.

Corporate bonds work just like gilts, but because companies, however big and bluechip they might be, are not as good a credit risk as the government, they must offer a higher interest rate than gilts to entice investors to put up their money. They will, naturally, try to get away with paying the very minimum. Bonds issued by the most financially secure companies will pay perhaps 25 basis points (0.25%) above a similar gilt, while less solid companies may have to pay upwards of 200 basis points (2%) more.

Who are they suitable for?

Bonds can be good investments for income-seeking investors, especially now that they can be put into an individual savings account (Isa), so investors can get the income tax-free. Anyone over the age of 18 can invest up to £7,000 a year in a maxi Isa containing such bonds. They can also switch monies held in previous years' Isas or Peps into corporate bonds. Anyone looking to increase the income yield from their portfolio at or around retirement should consider this option, especially if they have built up large holdings in equity-invested funds.

How to invest

You can buy corporate bonds directly, via a stockbroker, or invest in a corporate bond unit trust or open-ended investment company (known as an Oeic – basically, a more modern version of the unit trust). In either case, you can hold them within an Isa or a Pep. There are 80-odd specialist funds investing wholly or partly in corporate bonds – so how do you choose? There are a number of points to check:

- ◆ **Yield** Two figures will be quoted – an estimated annual, or running, yield, which shows the level of income investors can expect from the current portfolio, plus an estimated redemption yield, which takes into account the loss (or gain) to their capital if all the bonds in the portfolio are held until their maturity. The two figures are likely to be similar but are rarely identical. If the redemption yield is below the running yield, this means in effect that investors who withdraw all the income will be eating into their capital.

  At the time of writing, running yields on these funds varied between about 4% and 6%. The difference will be largely accounted for by the different bonds in which the managers decide to invest. There is a simple rule of thumb here. The higher the running yield, the more risky the underlying bonds are perceived to be by the stock market.

- ◆ **Charges** There is likely to be an initial charge, an annual management fee and possibly an exit charge as well. Competition has brought some charges down, but some products are still more expensive than others. Active investment management might provide better overall returns, but you will certainly benefit from lower charges.

- ◆ **Credit rating** Some managers promise they will invest only in bonds which are top-rated by the major credit rating agencies such as Standard & Poor's. Others cast their net more widely. The higher the interest rate, the more likelihood there is that one or more of the underlying securities will fail. If you want to invest in this area, do not put all your eggs into the single basket of higher yielding funds – spread it, with at least part of your holding in a lower yielding, higher rated fund.

Capital risk

Investors must be prepared to give up complete capital security if they invest in corporate bonds. There are three types of risk: first, and worst, there is the risk that the company will go into liquidation, in which case the bonds may be worthless. Some readers might remember the collapse of Barings Bank, when a number of private bondholders lost their entire capital. Buying through a bond fund effectively avoids this risk, because a fund is likely to hold the bonds of at least 20 companies (and probably many more) so that, at most, 5% of your capital is at risk if one company folds. Even if a company manages to stay afloat, the price of its bonds may drop if its financial state worsens, leading to fears that it could go bust some time in the future.

Second, the value of the bond or the fund will move from day to day as the market responds to changes in supply and demand or as underlying interest rates move up or down. Investing in a single bond will guarantee the level of income an investor receives during its life but will not fix the level of capital during that time.

Third, the higher the immediate income a fund provides, the more likely it is that the underlying bonds will be priced "over par". This means that one is effectively buying income at the expense of capital. The difference between the running, or annual, yield and the redemption yield is an indication of this.

Despite these caveats, corporate bonds are strong contenders for a place in the retirement portfolios of many investors, especially where they are held within the tax shelter of a Pep or an Isa, where the managers can reclaim the 20% tax paid on the interest.

Permanent interest-bearing shares (Pibs)

What they are

Building societies also need to raise capital from time to time, and the big ones are allowed to do so by issuing Pibs. In most respects, Pibs are similar to gilts and corporate bonds except that they are permanent. In other words, the society need never pay the capital back. Investors who want to get their money out must sell them on the stock market, where the price they receive will depend on interest rates at the time. Many of the Pibs in issue are from institutions such as the Halifax, which used to be building societies but have demutualised to become banks.

Who are they suitable for?

The attraction of Pibs is the level of income they pay. At the time of writing, they were paying about 7% gross, compared to 4.3% or thereabouts for a typical gilt.

Pibs cannot be put into a Pep or an Isa, so tax must be paid on the interest. However, couples planning their retirement portfolio might be able to arrange matters so that the partner who has little or no income (typically, the wife who has not built up a pension of her own) can hold the Pibs and escape with little or no tax to be paid. Pibs income is paid net of 20% tax. The one slight annoyance is that non-taxpayers must then claim back the tax from the Inland Revenue each year – there is no way to have it paid gross. Higher rate taxpayers must pay an additional 20%.

How to choose

Pibs cannot be bought directly from the issuing building society or bank; they must be bought via a stockbroker, who should be able to provide advice on the most suitable issues.

Capital risk

Pibs are not like ordinary building society investments as capital will fluctuate along with general interest rates and there is the remote risk that the issuer might go bust. Once bought, like any other fixed-interest security, the income stream is fixed. Because they are permanent, however, you cannot wait until maturity to be guaranteed the original capital back – you must take your chance in the market.

With-profits bonds

What they are

With-profits bonds are lump sum investments offered by life assurance companies. The with-profits fund is generally invested in a mixture of company shares, commercial property and gilts, making it a widely spread investment, though usually at least 60% to 70% is invested in shares. The funds are run with the aim of smoothing out returns from one year to the next by withholding some of the profits in good years to push up returns to policyholders during bad years. The bonds are in effect a lump sum version of the regular premium endowment policy, familiar to many from their mortgage paying days.

The life company declares a bonus each year, which is currently likely to be between 4% and 6% and bondholders can take an income of this level from the fund. The income will be net of basic rate tax, which cannot be reclaimed by non-taxpayers. Higher rate taxpayers may face an additional charge, but it is usually relatively low, as the tax rules allow bondholders to withdraw 5% a year of their original capital for a period of 20 years tax-free. If the underlying investments perform well, the company may also declare a one-off final bonus from time to time.

Who are they suitable for?

Anyone looking for a medium-risk investment which is a step or two up from a building society and which allows a regular income to be withdrawn, may find a with-profits bond appropriate.

They can be especially useful if you are caught in the age allowance trap, which applies to people aged over 65 whose income is (currently) somewhere between £17,600 and about £27,000. People in this situation have their extra age-related personal allowance withdrawn progressively at the rate of £1 for each £2 of extra income above £17,600 – which is equal to a basic tax rate of 33%. Because 5% a year can be withdrawn tax-free, income from a with-profits bond does not affect their age allowance.

Note that the bonds are essentially medium to long-term investments. If you cash in within the first five years, you may have to pay a surrender penalty, so they are not suitable for someone who might need their capital back in a hurry.

Capital security

The "income" payment is not quite what it seems, and should not be compared directly to a deposit account. The annual bonus represents the company's judgment of the likely return it will make that year, including interest and dividends received by the fund, plus capital growth.

If the fund's investments fail to meet the rate at which withdrawals are made, investors could be eating into their capital. Companies reserve the right to impose what is called a market value adjustment factor (MVAF) – a surrender penalty, which is imposed if you want to realise your investment at a time when the stock market is low. However, many companies promise that they will not impose this MVAF on the death of the bondholder and they may offer other guarantees as well – for example, that they will not impose it if you cash the bond in on the tenth anniversary of purchase.

How to choose

Investors need to take a number of factors into account before deciding which company's bond to buy. Least important is the size of the annual bonus – companies can choose to offer whatever rate they like. A higher rate simply means you are taking a greater risk if you withdraw all the bonus as income. You need to look at the overall strength of the company's reserves and its long-term record of paying out annual bonuses. It would be sensible to get independent advice before you buy. It could even save you money as some companies pay out huge amounts of commission – up to 6% – on these bonds. Buying direct won't mean you avoid this cost, but many independent advisers are prepared to rebate part of the initial commission to you if you buy through them.

Tax position on encashment

There may be some extra tax to pay when you cash in the bond. The calculation is a fairly complicated one known as top slicing. For a detailed explanation of this, turn to the following chapter and look under the section on life assurance bonds. In brief, extra tax is likely if you have made an overall profit on your investment and cash in the bond during a year when your income is above, or close to, the level at which higher rate tax starts to be charged.

What happens if you die

Most couples will hold the bonds in their joint names, which means they just carry on after the first partner dies. The bonds can be written in trust – a simple procedure – which can ensure that they are outside the inheritance tax net on death and the proceeds can be passed to your heirs without having to wait for probate.

Stock-market linked high income bonds

These bonds, which are always limited issues, offer some of the most enticing figures you will ever see before a % sign. They last for a fixed term – three to five years is typical – and the level of income is fixed and guaranteed during that time. So what's the catch? Simply, that while your income is secure, your capital is not. The bonds are linked to one or a number of stock market indices (or sometimes, a collection of individual shares) and you will receive your capital back intact only if the indices or share prices have performed to a minimum, pre-ordained level.

Technically, these bonds are life assurance vehicles which use the financial equivalent of smoke and mirrors to produce the end product – their inner workings can be extremely complex and it is not necessary to understand the minutiae of how they work. It is important, though, to realise the extent of the risk you could be taking. In the past, some of these bonds have provided excellent returns, but you should treat them with caution, especially if you are on a tight budget.

12

Higher-risk investments

All retirement portfolios should contain some investments which are capable of providing a growing income. Interest from banks and building societies will rise or fall over the years according to general interest rates; income from gilts and bonds will stay fixed at the level at which you bought them – which with hindsight may prove to be comfortably high or disastrously low. Apart from buying index-linked gilts, the principal way to protect your income against the effects of long-term inflation is to invest in equities – or company shares. This chapter covers:

- Buying shares
- Isas, Oeics, unit and investment trusts
- Investing for income
- Tax rules
- Life assurance bonds

Figure 2 shows how an income from shares can, over time, beat a cash deposit account by providing that all-important growth of income. The chart shows the ten-year record, starting in November 1991, of the average UK equity income unit trust compared to an investment in a building society account. It shows only what has happened to income payments, but the capital of the unit trust also rose during this time, while the sum invested in the building society, of course, stayed fixed.

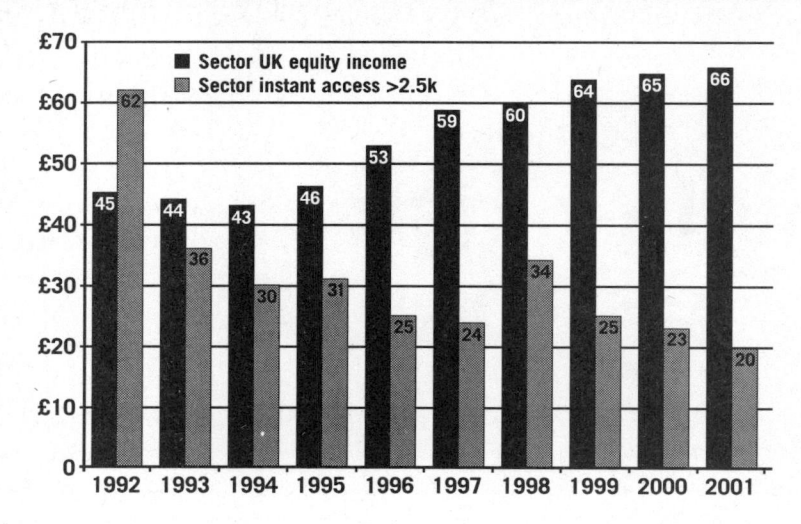

Higher-risk investments

Figure 2
UK equity income fund versus building society account, yearly income earned over each of ten years from a £1,000 lump sum. Figures to 1 November, 2001

Source: Autif

The younger people are when they retire, the more important it is for their portfolio to contain a significant element of "growing income" investments. For these people – anyone retiring around the age of 60 – there may be a case for having two retirement portfolios, one to see you through the first 15 years or thereabouts of your retirement, and the second to cater for your needs in later life, when a shift from equities towards fixed-interest investments may be appropriate – see chapter 14.

How to buy company shares

You can buy individual shares directly through a stockbroker or choose one of the pooled investment vehicles. The main ones are unit trusts, open-ended investment companies (known as Oeics – basically, a more modern version of the unit trust) and investment trusts. However you buy the shares, you can put them into an individual savings account – an Isa – a tax-free wrapper which shelters your investment from all capital gains tax and from most income tax.

Individual savings accounts

Anyone over the age of 16 can take out a cash Isa each year, but you must be 18 to open an equity Isa. The maximum that can be invested in any one year is £7,000. You can choose up to three mini Isas or one maxi Isa; you cannot have both. Details of the rules are given on page 105. Note: if you go down the mini Isa route, you can choose three managers, one for each type of investment. If you choose a maxi Isa, you are restricted to a single plan manager.

Peps and Isas in a retirement portfolio

Many readers of this book will already have some money invested in Isas or their predecessors, Peps (personal equity plans). Because of their tax advantages, they are practically a "no-brainer" – if you are going to invest in unit or investment trusts, you should, without question, do so via the Isa. With unit trusts, at any rate, there is usually no cost to investing via an Isa. In fact, the reverse is often true – the charges are lower if you invest through the Isa rather than buying the trust direct. With investment trusts or a direct holding of shares, using an Isa does usually cost extra but the charges are relatively low.

The big advantage is that it gives you the great freedom of knowing that you can rearrange your portfolio at any time without facing a hefty capital gains tax bill – and, perhaps, a hefty bill from your accountant for working out your liability. The immediate income tax advantage may seem of less significance if you are using the Pep or Isa for investing in shares, especially if you are a basic rate taxpayer, as their initial yield is relatively low and only the 10% tax on dividends can be reclaimed. Higher rate taxpayers fare better, as if they held shares outside a Pep or Isa, they would have to pay extra tax on the dividends.

The government has stated that this 10% tax reclaim will last only until 2004, after which it may be abolished. We will have to wait and see.

In recent years, the investment constraints which applied to Peps have been lifted. Originally, unit and investment trusts had to be at least 50% invested in UK or other European Community shares to qualify for the full £6,000 a year investment in a general Pep. It was also possible to invest £3,000 each year in a single company Pep. Both rules have been abolished so it is now possible to rearrange your Pep holdings, perhaps achieving a wider spread, while keeping safely within the original Pep tax shelter.

Deciding to use an Isa for future investment is only the first step. You must now decide what investments to buy.

Unit trusts

Unit trusts are pooled investments which usually invest in at least 40 shares and often many more. Each unit holder gets a slice of the whole investment. Like other pooled vehicles, their main advantage is in providing a spread of risk which is hard to match by investing directly in shares, unless you have very substantial funds. In addition, good fund managers can add considerable value by managing the investments well – though it has to be said, only a minority do so consistently.

Their disadvantage, one shared to a great or lesser extent with all types of share investment, is their cost. Typically, unit trusts have an initial charge of 5% to 5.5% and an annual management charge of 1% to 1.75%, though some are cheaper. Charges are automatically deducted from the investment. New investors also face the "spread" – the difference between buying and selling prices on the shares in the underlying portfolio. In all, this generally means there is a gap of perhaps 6% between the buying and selling prices for the units on the same day.

Initial charges on unit trust Isas are often less than this – often only 3% as compared to 5%, although a few make a "back end" charge if you cash them in within the first five years.

Open-ended investment companies (Oeics)

These have identical investment characteristics to unit trusts but differ in their charging structure. The principal difference is that they ignore the spread on the underlying shares and there is one price for buying and selling units in the fund.

Oeics are a product of European harmonisation. Many management companies have already converted their funds from unit trusts to Oeics and no doubt others will follow. This will make practically no difference to the investor and the two vehicles are treated as one for the purpose of performance statistics.

Investing for a growing income

There are literally thousands of different unit trusts and Oeics available, covering every conceivable investment specialisation. Some are run with the aim of producing maximum capital growth, totally ignoring income. Others go for total return – hoping to achieve good profits through a mixture of growth and income, and others still concentrate on providing a decent level of income. These last are the ones which may interest retired investors in particular.

There are various types of income fund. The Association of Unit Trusts and Investment Funds has the following categories:

- ◆ **UK equity income** These funds invest at least 80% of their assets in UK equities and aim for more than 110% of the yield of the FTSE All-Share index.
- ◆ **Global equity income** These funds invest at least 80% of their assets in equities (but no more than 80% of that in UK equities) and aim for a yield in excess of 110% of the FT World index.
- ◆ **UK equity and bond income** These funds invest at least 80% of their assets in the UK, between 20% and 80% in fixed-interest securities and the balance in equities. They aim for at least 120% of the yield on the FTSE All-Share index.

There are also three categories for funds investing in UK fixed-interest securities:

- ◆ **UK corporate bond** This category contains trusts which invest mostly in high-rated corporate bonds.
- ◆ **UK other bond** This contains funds which invest in lower-rated bonds and may contain preference shares and convertibles.
- ◆ **UK gilt** These invest in government securities.

There are numerous other specialist categories, but for income-seeking investors, these are likely to be the most important, along with the UK all companies sector, which aims broadly to match the All-Share index and includes index-tracking funds.

Table 19 provides a summary of the current yields and average past performance over various periods for these categories. It also shows some benchmark figures – inflation over the period, along with the results of an investment in building societies and the performance of the FTSE All-Share index.

Table 19
Unit trusts: past performance and current income yields

Category	Value of £1,000 invested – years ago			Current average yield
	1	5	10	
UK equity income	£851	£1,395	£2,533	3.6%
Global equity income	£697	£1,376	£2,301	1.7%
UK equity and bond income	£897	£1,057	£2,396	4.0%
UK corporate bond	£1,048	£1,400	£2,132	4.9%
UK other bond	£975	£1,411	£2,546	6.3%
UK gilt	£1,030	£1,376	£1,932	3.3%
UK all companies	£757	£1,308	£2,412	1.4%
FTSE All-Share index	£806	£1,407	£2,637	
Building society	£1,034	£1,227	£1,575	
RPI	£1,017	£1,135	£1,292	

Results represent the average fund. All figures include reinvestment of income net of basic rate tax and are after deduction of relevant charges.
All figures to 1 November, 2001

Source: Money Management

Income funds: how to choose

The level of charges, the current yield and the past performance of the fund are key criteria for choosing an income trust. Investors could also look at when particular trusts pay out their income.

Charges

Investors should check the annual management charge in particular, because this is usually deducted from the income before it is paid out. Equity income funds are long-term investments; someone putting their money in at age 60 could be holding it for 15 years or even longer (as long as it remains competently managed) and, while initial charges are a pain, the effect of the annual management charge makes itself felt cumulatively over time. Some income funds have annual charges of 1% or less, while others charge 1.5% a year or more.

Yield

Current yields on UK equity income funds vary from about 2% to 5%. The highest is not necessarily the best. Funds which offer a higher than average starting yield achieve this in one of two ways.

The first is to include a significant proportion of fixed-interest and convertible stocks within the portfolio. Although these pay a higher starting income, they have little or no scope for producing growth in that income, so their long-term prospects may not be so good.

The second is to choose higher yielding ordinary shares. But there is usually a good reason why yields on certain shares are much higher than others. It means the stock market has marked down the prices of those shares. Now, that might be simply because the company has fallen on (temporary) hard times or has fallen out of favour with the market. Or it might be because the market has got it right in assessing that the outlook for the company, its profits and future dividends, is poor. If the stock market is wrong, investors benefit – they get the high yield now, plus capital profits when the company's share price recovers. Some fund managers have done very well in the past by adopting this approach – but others have not been so clever or lucky.

Past performance

There is considerable debate among the financial regulators about the extent to which investors should take heed of the past performance of funds. In one sense, of course, past performance is misleading. The fact that total returns from the UK stock market averaged nearly 20% a year for the 20 years up to 1999, or that cash deposits paid an average of around 8% during that time, is neither here nor there as regards immediate future prospects. But it seems common sense to say that some people are better at managing funds than others and, at the very least, you want to make sure that you are not putting your money with someone who has proved over time that he is basically a duffer.

Payment dates of dividends

Most trusts pay out dividends twice a year, although a few offer monthly income. If you want income more regularly than twice a year, you can construct a portfolio of four or five trusts, so receiving dividend distributions maybe eight times a year. Financial advisers usually recommend that investors should be prepared to be flexible and not insist on regular monthly payouts, because this could mean choosing trusts solely on their payment dates rather than more important characteristics.

Is it worth getting independent advice on funds?

Yes is the short answer. Good firms of advisers are constantly monitoring the funds' performances and when individual managers move from one group to another. They do not always get it right, but you might as well choose from a position of knowledge.

Spreading the risk

While income may be the prime aim of a typical retirement portfolio, it is a good idea, assuming you have sufficient funds, to spread your money more widely, especially in the early years of retirement. That means going for funds that aim for growth as well as income, perhaps invested in different parts of the world as well as the UK. One option is a tracker fund, whose aim is to match an index of shares such as the FTSE All-Share. Because no active management is involved, charges are much lower. You should not have to pay an initial charge and annual management fees can be as low as 0.3%.

Investment trusts

Investment trusts are pooled investments designed, like unit trusts, to provide a spread of risk for those with relatively small amounts to invest. However, unlike unit trusts or Oeics, they are limited companies, quoted on the Stock Exchange. The oldest trust was set up in the 1850s and many of the big general trusts were incorporated in the 19th or early 20th centuries.

There are two essential differences between unit and investment trusts from the investor's point of view. First is gearing. Investment trusts are allowed to borrow to invest. Managers are likely to do this if they think the prospects for investing in their chosen stock market are so good that they will make a profit even after paying interest on the borrowed money. If the managers are right, this gearing is good news for investors, but if they are wrong, investors will be in a worse position than if their trust had no gearing at all.

Second is volatility. Because investment trusts are quoted companies, their share price is influenced not just by the value of their underlying investments, but also by the levels of supply and demand for the trusts' shares. Ten or 15 years ago, investment trusts were unfashionable and no-one wanted to buy their shares. As a result, their share prices stood on big discounts to their underlying assets. Then that changed, trusts became popular and the discount narrowed and in some cases disappeared altogether. Occasionally, their share prices even stood at a premium to their underlying assets. People who bought when discounts were high benefited from the narrowing of the discount.

Since then, discounts have widened a bit and then narrowed again. Latterly, trusts have made great efforts to minimise volatility by buying back shares when the discount gets too large. Nevertheless, investment trusts are always likely to be more volatile than unit trusts and Oeics.

So why should anyone consider investing in investment trusts? There are three basic reasons. First, charges are relatively low. Some of the big old trusts charge well under 0.5% annually for active management – a third or less than typical unit trust charges. Second, you might get better performance, if the managers get their gearing decisions right. Third, if you are considering investing in less liquid areas, such as smaller companies, or some of the smaller stock markets in the world, investment trusts have an edge

If an investor wants to sell investment trust shares, he must sell them on the Stock Exchange to another investor – he does not sell them back to the company. This means the fund manager does not have to grapple with a fund that is ballooning or shrinking in size (as a unit trust manager must do). He is not forced to sell his best investments merely to meet the flood of redemptions as the unit trust manager sometimes does.

Variations on the investment trust theme

A number of investment trusts are set up on a split-capital basis. This means that their share capital is divided into different types of share. The simplest split is between income shares, which get all the income from a portfolio but none of the capital growth, and capital shares, which get all the growth but none of the income. If the split between the two types of share is equal, income shareholders get an income of twice the going rate, and that should grow over the years matching the general growth in profits and dividends. All split-capital trusts have a redemption date at which time they are broken up and the assets distributed to shareholders according to their entitlements.

The income-capital type of split is the most straightforward. Many split trusts are more complicated – in one case, not so long ago, a trust had something like 13 share classes. Understanding exactly how they work and the precise degree of potential risk and reward can get extremely complicated, especially when those trusts make a practice of investing in the shares of other split-capital trusts. If you are interested in this area, it is vital to get professional advice.

Investment trusts: how to choose

The Association of Investment Trust Companies provides a raft of literature on how trusts work and their past performance, along with details of current discounts or premiums and the level of gearing for each trust.

Many firms of private client stockbrokers will offer advice on investment trusts, but if you are happy to decide for yourself, you can in most cases buy direct as trust management companies offer low-cost schemes for buying or selling their shares. Many management companies also operate their own Pep and Isa schemes so you can put new money into an Isa investment trust or transfer funds held within a Pep.

Tax on Oeics, unit and investment trusts

Investments made through a Pep or an Isa are not liable to income or capital gains tax. If you invest directly, dividend income is paid net of a 10% tax charge which satisfies basic rate tax liability – higher rate taxpayers must declare the income on their tax return and pay extra.

Capital gains realised within the trust are tax-free. When investors sell their holdings, they are potentially liable to capital gains tax on any profits, although they can set their annual exemption (£7,500 in the 2001-02 tax year) against their profits. If you hold the trust until you die, no CGT is payable at that point, but the total proceeds are part of your estate and your heirs may have to pay inheritance tax.

This freedom from CGT makes these investments a more attractive proposition than life assurance bonds (see below).

Life assurance bonds

Single premium life assurance-linked bonds are another form of pooled investment aimed at private investors. Like the others, they provide a spread of risk and professional management. Their charges are similar to those of unit trusts.

The with-profits bonds detailed in the previous chapter are one form of these. Others are unit-linked, which means they invest in funds similar to unit trusts where the value of the bond depends directly on the value of the underlying investment – there is no smoothing effect as there is in with-profits bonds.

A distribution bond invests in a managed fund, including equities, property and fixed-interest securities, and is one step up the risk ladder from a with-profits bond. It has a similar investment mix but there are no reserves to smooth out returns. Other bonds may be linked to an underlying fund investing wholly in equities and their risk profile will be basically the same as for unit trusts investing in similar stocks.

The difference between bonds and trusts is not so much their underlying investments, but the way they are treated for tax. Because they are technically life assurance investments, they are, on the whole, taxed more heavily than unit trusts. But they do have an advantage for people caught in the age allowance trap where the higher age-related personal allowance is progressively withdrawn once income exceeds £17,600. The main tax rules are as follows:

- ◆ Income arising within the bond is taxed at the basic rate, which cannot be reclaimed by non-taxpayers. Higher rate taxpayers do not face any immediate further charge, but see below.
- ◆ Up to 5% of the bond's original value may be withdrawn by investors for up to 20 years, free of tax. This counts as return of capital. This allowance can be carried forward so that, if nothing is withdrawn for the first ten years, a total of 10% may be withdrawn for the following ten years. Any withdrawals above this limit are free of extra tax for basic rate taxpayers but attract an additional tax charge in the hands of higher rate taxpayers.
- ◆ Capital gains realised within the bond are taxed at the level of basic rate tax (22%), which is automatically deducted from the value of the holdings. Investors cannot use their own annual CGT allowance to set against these gains.
- ◆ When the bond is sold, basic rate taxpayers have nothing more to pay. Higher rate taxpayers face a further 18% charge on the profits. To establish the extent of this liability, the proceeds from the sale are added to any earlier withdrawals. The original purchase price is then deducted from the total and the resulting amount – in effect the total profit (irrespective of whether it comes from reinvested income or capital growth) is divided by the number of years the investor has

held the bond. That sum is added to the investor's income for the year in question, to establish whether it would give rise to a higher rate tax liability. If it does, the whole of the profit is taxed at higher rate minus basic rate tax – in other words, 40% minus 22%, or 18%.

This rather complicated procedure is known as top slicing. It generally means that the bonds are more heavily taxed than unit trusts, but it can work to investors' advantage. For instance, if you are a higher rate taxpayer now, but anticipate that your rate will fall after retirement to the basic rate, you can delay cashing in the bond until then, so there will be no extra tax to pay.

Investing directly in shares

Some investors prefer to invest directly in company shares rather than managed funds. Given the need to spread risk among a number of companies, the minimum investment required to make this a sensible move is £50,000 – and if you want a firm of stockbrokers to manage your portfolio, it may well suggest a much higher figure.

Investing directly does not, of course, mean going without the tax advantages of Isas – or Peps, if you already have them. Many stockbrokers run their own share-only Isa and Pep plans, and either manage the underlying investment for you or offer a "self-select" Isa where you make the choice of shares. There will be fees attached – if you decide on a self-select plan, check these before you sign up.

13

Investment planning in practice

Investors should treat this chapter with some caution. Its purpose is not to tell you precisely where you should be putting your money now, but to provide an idea of the sort of investments you probably ought to have at retirement.

At any given time there is, of course, no single answer to this, because so much depends on you: how much you have to invest, the size of your pension, your liabilities and your general attitude to investment.

To this range of variables one could add countless others: do you intend to move house, either soon or later? Are you retiring in your mid fifties or your late sixties? Do you want to leave significant sums to your children? Do you expect to be beneficiaries from the estates of your parents or other relatives?

These factors should be taken into account by a competent financial adviser. Only after assessing all of them would he or she suggest a portfolio, based on investment conditions prevailing at that time. Despite these caveats, it is worth putting some flesh on the bones of the generalisations made so far. And it is fair to say that, although the details will inevitably be different, if your circumstances are something like one of the five examples that follow, the structure of your portfolio ought to be something like the solution suggested.

The characteristics of a good portfolio

If you undergo a similar exercise, it is worth taking a step back from the final recommendations and asking the following questions:
- Does the portfolio meet all your needs?
- If not, does it meet the most important needs and are the reasons why they cannot all be met sensible ones?
- Are you happy with the level of risk it involves?
- Does it build in enough flexibility to cope with reasonable emergencies?
- Does it ensure you have enough liquid funds?
- Does it involve a proper spread of risk?
- Will it take care of longer-term requirements as well as the immediate future?
- Do you understand fully why the recommendations have been made and the nature of the investments involved?

If you are happy that the answer to all these questions is yes, then that is the hallmark of a job well done.

The following "solutions" have been provided by five different independent financial advisers.

Scenario 1

The problem

Arthur Clough, aged 62, is retiring on a final salary pension of £14,000 a year from a medium-sized company. His wife, Mary, is 59. The scheme has lately been paying out inflation matching increases to pensioners but this has been on an ex-gratia basis.

He can take the full pension or tax-free cash of £33,000 with a reduced pension of £11,000 a year. Mary gave up her job a year ago and has no pension entitlement other than the basic state pension, which will provide slightly more on her own record (£2,100 a year) than by claiming on her husband's.

They are good money managers but cautious by nature and a little worried about how they will fare in retirement. They own their home and would like, eventually, to leave something to their children but they see no need to make any special plans to do so.

Their investments are:
- £25,000 in building society accounts
- £5,000 in a Tessa-only Isa
- £3,000 in popular shares including BT and Halifax

Their only immediate spending plans are for a holiday costing up to £2,000. Should they take the lump sum from the pension? If so, where should they invest it?

A solution

Provided by Patrick Connolly of Chartwell Investment Management, independent financial advisers

The tax-free lump sum is one of the most attractive features of a pension policy, especially because if Arthur does not take this, he will be taxed on the income it produces from the pension.

That said, Arthur and Mary are concerned about how they will fare in retirement. If they take the £33,000 tax-free lump sum they will lose £3,000 a year in income. It is possible this £3,000 would also rise in line with inflation, compounding the loss. To generate £3,000 a year, they would need a return of more than 9% on the £33,000 lump sum.

A purchased life annuity will generate an income of that order, especially considering that not all of the returns from this are taxable, as a portion will be deemed to be return of capital. However, if it seems likely that his company pension will rise with inflation, the logical option is to take the full pension and not the tax-free cash. It will need to be checked whether Arthur's pension provides an income for Mary in the event of his death.

To pay for their holiday and, more importantly, to ensure they have adequate provision for retirement, they need to assess their existing investments.

First, they need to ensure that they have enough money easily accessible on deposit to cater for any unforeseen events. This amount will vary from individual to individual but £10,000 would be reasonable. This should be held solely in Mary's name as, with her level of income, she will be a non-taxpayer, whereas Arthur's pension will mean that he is a taxpayer.

After ensuring that £10,000 is easily accessible, Arthur and Mary have £15,000 on deposit. There is nothing wrong with this approach if they are particularly cautious and, again, they should ensure that it is held in Mary's name, as she will still be a non-taxpayer. With this money, they should look for accounts that give less access but offer higher returns. For example, 90-day accounts or, ideally, fixed-term accounts from one to five years.

It appears that neither utilises their annual Isa allowance. They should start moving the surplus money they have on deposit into mini cash Isas. They will each be able to invest £3,000 a year, gaining tax-free returns in excess of normal building society accounts. If at some stage the £10,000 easily accessible money is also moved into mini cash Isas, they need to allow easy access to capital with no penalties.

Arthur and Mary may also consider stakeholder pensions. Regardless of their earnings, they can each put £2,808 a year into a stakeholder pension plan and this amount, with tax relief, will be increased to £3,600. They can turn these plans into income (a process known as "vesting") whenever they wish, though the younger they are, the lower the income they are likely to receive and this income would be taxable for Arthur.

The £3,000 worth of shares they hold appear to be doing very little for them. Also, holding individual shares does seem to be out of line with their cautious nature. They should sell them and use the proceeds to fund their holiday. Any leftover money could be used as a contribution to their first cash Isa.

Scenario 2

The problem

Thomas Gray is self-employed and decides to retire at 65. His wife, Vivien, is five years younger. He has built up £100,000 in personal pensions. His options are to take a level pension of £7,240, one increasing at 5% a year with a starting level of £4,100, or an inflation-linked pension starting at £5,110. In each case, the pension will reduce by a third after his death.

Alternatively, he can take a cash sum from the fund – a maximum of £25,000, which will leave his pension options at £5,430 (level), £3,075 (increasing at 5%) or £3,833 (inflation linked). Once again, all figures include a two-thirds widow's pension.

As well as the personal pension, Thomas qualifies for the full basic state pension of £6,026 a year plus a Serps entitlement of £535 a year. Vivien has no pension income of her own.

The Gray's other investments are:
- £22,000 in building society accounts held in Thomas's name
- £5,000 in a building society account in Vivien's name, where the interest is paid gross
- £10,200 in a Tessa due to mature in a few months
- £6,800 in a life assurance linked managed bond

Thomas and Vivien would like an income of £800 a month after tax but could manage on less. They need to replace their car shortly and are mentally setting aside £5,000 (perhaps from the proceeds of the Tessa) to do so. What sort of pension should they take? And where should their money be invested?

A solution

Provided by Amanda Davidson of Holden Meehan, independent financial advisers

The biggest threat for any investment portfolio is not short-term volatility but long-term inflation. So, Thomas and Vivien should take the tax-free cash and opt for an inflation-linked pension, which will start at £3,833 a year. This includes a two-thirds widow's pension – an important point, given that Vivien does not have a pension of her own. The state and personal pension between them should provide a net monthly income of £804, meeting the Grays' target figure, though it would be wise to aim for a little more – perhaps an extra £50 a month – to cover emergencies.

This can be achieved by using £12,000 of his cash sum to invest in new pension plans, which are then immediately turned into annuities. This is probably best done by spreading the investment over two tax years, in each of which Thomas and Vivien can take out a stakeholder plan (both are entitled to pay in up to £3,600 gross each tax year, meaning a net payment in each case of £2,808). The majority of the money should be put into a stakeholder in Vivien's name, so the pension income will be tax-free, as she is not using her personal allowance.

If they want, they can take out a quarter of the total investment – £3,000 – as cash, making the net cost (after tax relief) a little over £6,000.

These stakeholder pensions will, at current rates, buy them inflation-linked pensions of about £600 gross, £540 a year net if Vivien's stakeholder plan takes the maximum contribution of £3,600 gross for two years, or a little less if the investment is split equally into stakeholders for both.

Having sorted out the income question, we now have a free hand regarding the rest of the Gray's investments.

These are:
◆ £27,000 in building societies
◆ £15,640 in pension cash (including the tax relief)
◆ £10,200 Tessa
◆ £6,800 managed bond

The money should be invested as follows:

Investment	Amount	Held by
Car money in building society	£5,000	Vivien
Building society	£5,000	Vivien
National Savings index-linked certificates	£5,000	Thomas
Individual savings account	£6,000	Thomas
Unit trusts	£25,000	Vivien or jointly
Managed bond	£6,800	Jointly
With-profits bond	£6,840	Jointly

◆ **Building society investments** Some money must be set aside for emergencies, and should be held in Vivien's name, along with the car money, so she can get the interest gross. There is little point in reinvesting in a Tessa-only Isa.
◆ **National Savings certificates** The current issue (the 21st) provides 1.75% plus inflation, guaranteed for five years and tax-free, making it a secure investment and a good hedge should inflation rise markedly.
◆ **Isas and unit trusts** These investments are to provide capital growth with a view to providing an income in the future in case there are additional costs when the Grays are older. The Isa, being tax-free, should be in Thomas's name; the rest should be held either jointly or in Vivien's name.

The unit trust holdings should be split as follows: 40% in the UK, 25% in Europe, 20% in the US and 15% in general international funds.

They should be growth orientated trusts, providing little in the way of income now, but may be switched later to income producing investments. These are long-term investments and should be held for at least five years.
- **The managed bond** If the Grays are happy with its past performance, they might as well keep it. If it has not done so well, they should cash it and add the proceeds to their unit trust portfolio.
- **The with-profits bond** This type of investment evens out the troughs and peaks of the equity market – particularly important when there is high volatility. Bonuses once added form part of the contact. Although reasonably secure, the provider may apply a market value adjustment factor when the bond is cashed in, which means there is no guarantee that the capital is protected. However, the factor is likely to be applied only if the bond is cashed in during a bad time on the stock market.

Overall, the Grays have a comfortable income to live on, which means they can afford to look ahead and to take on some risk with a view to securing capital growth potential for the future, by means of a good, well-balanced portfolio of equities.

Scenario 3

The problem

George Herbert retires at 61 with a company pension of £25,000 a year and a cash sum of £100,000. He and his wife Anne, aged 58, have an extensive investment portfolio, built up somewhat haphazardly over the years.

Between them, they have:
- £60,000 in growth-orientated Peps and Isas largely invested in the UK
- £20,000 in European Peps
- £18,000-plus in Tessa-only Isas
- £30,000 in building societies, in Anne's name
- £8,000 in a high-interest cheque account – the proceeds of an endowment policy which they have yet to invest
- £4,000 in a Japanese unit trust

They would like an additional £5,000 or more income to spend but are keen to retain the potential for growth. They live in a house worth around £400,000, which is fairly expensive to run. They anticipate moving at some stage but have no definite plans. They would like to be able to leave reasonably substantial funds to their children. They have decided to take the lump sum and have earmarked £10,000 of this for immediate spending. Where should they invest the rest to meet their needs?

A solution

Provided by Mark Dampier of Hargreaves Lansdown, independent financial advisers

George and Anne will have capital of around £240,000 to invest once they retire, less the £10,000 required for short-term spending. Their existing portfolio is quite well spread, but a shift in emphasis from growth towards income will help provide the extra money they require. £14,000 from their liquid capital should be invested in corporate bond Isas, while £10,000 of their existing growth Peps should be switched into the same investments. The remaining UK growth Peps and Isas should be switched to UK equity income funds (still within the Pep or Isa) and perhaps, in due course, the European Peps could be similarly transferred – it will depend on the couple's future needs for income.

Meanwhile, Anne should continue holding her £30,000 in a building society account for the time being, together with £8,000 in the high-interest cheque account. This may be useful for future years' Isa allowances. £40,000 from the cash sum should be placed in a portfolio of equity income funds in Anne's name – the total income from these three sources should use most of her tax-free personal allowance. A further £25,000 should be placed in a commercial property fund which is a low to medium-risk investment and should allow the couple to take out 5% a year tax-free without involving much risk to the remaining capital. The Tessa-only Isas should be retained.

The Japanese unit trust should be sold and the proceeds added to the balance of £11,000 and invested in a managed portfolio of international growth-orientated unit and investment trusts. This should generate capital growth and provide the means to invest in Isas in later years, perhaps with a switch to income producing investments, depending on whether the couple feel the need for extra income.

Regarding inheritance tax, they are really too young to consider serious planning, although they might consider starting a whole life assurance policy written in absolute trust for the children, which would provide an immediate cash sum to meet all, or a part, of any future tax liability. They should also ensure their wills are up-to-date and provide maximum flexibility should a deed of family arrangement be appropriate on the first death.

Overall, this investment portfolio produces income of about £8,000 a year, most of which will be free of tax. More importantly, £90,000 of the total is committed to equity income funds, which should provide both a growing income and some prospects of capital growth over the years, while a further £25,000 is also in equities.

Investment	Amount
Anne's portfolio	
Tessa-only Isa	£ 9,000
Building society	£30,000
High interest cheque account	£ 8,000
European Peps	£10,000
Corporate bond Peps and Isas	£12,000
Equity income Peps	£25,000
Equity income funds	£40,000
Commercial property bond	£25,000
George's portfolio	
Tessa-only Isa	£ 9,000
European Pep	£10,000
Corporate bond Pep and Isas	£12,000
Equity income Pep	£25,000
Growth portfolio	£15,000
Total	**£230,000**

Scenario 4

The problem

Liz Barrett, aged 60, retires after many years as personal assistant to the managing director of a small manufacturing and exporting company on a final salary of £20,000. For much of her life she made no pension savings, but in the last ten years has been putting money into a personal pension on a regular basis. The fund is now worth £60,000.

She owns her own flat which is fully paid for. However, the service charges have shown a worrying tendency to increase well above inflation in the last few years. Having helped her company in the struggle to remain competitive in world markets through the high inflation of the 1970s and 1980s, Liz is very conscious of the need for protection against future inflation.

In addition to her pension savings, she has £30,000 in building society accounts, mostly on short notice. She will qualify for the full single person's old age pension and has some Serps entitlement as well. Her pension fund will buy her a pension of approximately £4,074 on a level basis but just £2,770 index-linked. If she wants to take the maximum tax-free cash of £15,000, her pension would be £3,055 level or £2,079 index-linked.

A solution

Provided by Ian Millward of Chase de Vere Investments, independent financial advisers

With the Bank of England aiming to keep inflation at about 2.5%, there may be a strong temptation for people today not to index-link their pension.

However, Liz is absolutely right to identify inflation as her number one enemy. There are definitely no crystal balls, so while a return to the inflation levels of the 1970s and 1980s seems unlikely, who knows where we'll be in ten or 15 years? Given the fact that Liz's personal pension will be a significant part of her overall income, it doesn't pay to take chances.

No-one could criticise her if she decided not to take the tax-free cash and make the most of her pension now. However, I think she would also benefit from the flexibility of having access to more of her money, so she should take the maximum tax-free cash of £15,000, which will leave her with a pension of only £2,079. A happy compromise would be to use some of this cash to fund a stakeholder pension.

In Liz's position, it is crucial to build in as much flexibility as possible. Moving into retirement is a new experience and it will take some time for her to settle into her new lifestyle and income requirements. The peace of mind of knowing she can increase her spending is important, but if she doesn't need this, it is important that she can reinvest her income to provide as much extra growth as possible for the future.

Assuming she takes £15,000 as tax-free cash, Liz will have £45,000 available for investment. Initially, I think, she should opt to keep more money on hand than she's likely to need. After all, it's far easier in a year's time to decide to invest a little more than to find she has not kept back enough and needs to cash in investments at a bad time. I recommend she keeps up to £10,000 in a cash deposit account, but she should check the savings tables in the quality national press and on Teletext to make sure she's getting the best rate. If she has access to the internet, she is likely to find that an online account will best serve her purposes.

With the remaining £35,000, she should aim for investments that can pay a reasonable level of income but have the flexibility to provide some growth. In this tax year, £7,000 should be invested in a corporate bond Isa. A corporate bond is essentially a loan to a company and the rate of return depends on its credit worthiness. That's why it's important that cautious investors aren't seduced by some of the high headline rates on offer. Typically, a fund producing a yield of around 7% should strike a balance between income and reasonable capital security. By taking this out through an Isa, Liz will get these returns tax-free. She should do the same after April to make the most of both this year's and next year's Isa allowances.

She should invest a further a £9,000 in a UK equity income fund. This will invest predominantly in the shares of UK companies, so she needs to be aware that the value of these can fall quite sharply at times. However, over a five or ten-year period they should deliver good returns. Liz will also have the option of taking an income, probably in the region of 3% net and, while this isn't huge to start with, as the fund grows in value, it can become increasingly worthwhile. It should also be possible in future years to switch this fund over to an Isa (subject to the limit of £7,000 in any one tax year) and get these returns tax-free.

A further £10,000 should be invested in a with-profits bond. These look to smooth the returns from the stock market and pay these out as a steady bonus. As stock market returns have been quite poor recently, they have come in for some criticism and you are placing a lot of trust in the life companies that issue them to maintain bonuses. Nevertheless, they can be good investments and Liz just needs to be sure that the company she invests in is financially strong and, therefore, able to maintain good levels of bonuses during tough years. I would suggest she draws out an income of 5% net from the bond, which should leave a little room for growth. With-profits bonds offer flexibility – she can either take the income or leave it re-invested for growth so they suit her situation very well.

This leaves a balance of £2,000, which can be used to fund a stakeholder pension from which she can take an immediate annuity. If she funds £2,000 initially, she will receive tax relief making this up to £2,564. She can then withdraw 25% as a tax-free lump sum (£641) and buy an annuity with the balance. In effect, she is buying an annuity for £1,923 but only paying £1,359 for it. This could generate a net income of about £100 a year.

Overall, Liz needs to remember that there is no single perfect investment, which is why she should have a good spread and then be prepared to invest over a five-year period. However, overall this is a low to medium-risk approach, which should allow her to achieve much better returns than she might get from the bank or building society, as well as a decent level of income without the full risk of stock market investment.

Liz's portfolio

Investment	Amount	Income net
Cash deposit	£10,000	£420
Corporate bond Isa	£7,000	£500
Corporate bond Isa	£7,000	£500
UK equity income fund	£9,000	£270
With-profits bond	£10,000	£500
Stakeholder pension	£2,000	£140
Total	**£45,000**	**£2,330**

Scenario 5

The problem

Christopher Smart, a partner in a firm of management consultants, earns £80,000 a year. He has decided to retire two years early at the age of 58. He has personal pension funds totalling £464,000, invested in managed funds. His wife Jane, who is three years younger, works part-time in an art gallery and has no intention of stopping work for the time being. Her income is relatively low – about £8,000 a year – and is, in any case, "hers" and not to be taken into account in his planning.

In addition to the pension fund, Christopher has an equity portfolio worth £138,000. Much of it was inherited from his mother, who died three years ago, and represents a collection of shares, unit and investment trusts built up by his father over the years. He admits the portfolio could probably do with an overhaul and would like an adviser to recommend an "ideal" medium-risk portfolio which he could compare with what he actually has, making such changes as he sees fit. A further £30,000 is held in various Peps.

While he is formally retiring, Christopher expects to be working as a consultant. Indeed, he is discussing a project which may come to fruition in about nine months and could be very lucrative – a fee of £100,000 is on the table for the work which would last about a year. Meanwhile, he needs income – he reckons about £2,000 a month after tax – but with flexibility as well.

The Smarts' other investments:
- £18,000 in Tessa-only Isas
- £47,000 in building societies which they would like to keep – whether tax efficient or not – because they have recently acquired a "cow shed" in France which needs extensive modernisation.

A solution

Provided by John Turton of Best Invest, independent financial advisers

There are three priorities for Christopher:
- Making up his income shortfall until his anticipated consultancy project starts
- Reviewing his existing portfolio
- Utilising his and his wife's tax allowances

Income shortfall There are two possible routes for making up the £2,000 per month income shortfall. The first is to encash some of the equity portfolio he has inherited from his mother. Given the fact that these investments have been held for only three years, and he anticipates needing £18,000 over the next nine months, it is likely that this can be done without incurring capital gains tax through the use of annual allowances. The restructuring of his largely inherited portfolio will probably involve encashments anyway. However, if the consultancy project doesn't emerge on the expected timescale or falls through, this solution may not be ideal.

A better option may be to begin a "phased drawdown" of retirement benefits. Since April 2001 personal pensions can be subdivided into numerous arrangements, allowing partial selection of retirement benefits rather than having to opt for all or nothing. For example, Christopher could ring-fence £64,000 of his total pension pool and under the personal pension rules he could then draw 25% (£16,000) as a tax-free cash sum. The remaining £48,000 could be used for a pension fund drawdown.

As a 58-year-old male, the maximum income that should be selected in advance is £3,456 a year, which at Christopher's current 40% income tax rate would reduce to £2,073 (although the tax deduction may be lower if the nine-month hiatus falls in a single tax year). The combination of this income with the cash lump sum would cover the expected £18,000 income shortfall for the next nine months. The remaining pension fund drawdown monies of £44,544 will remain invested for growth. Drawdown is preferable to buying an annuity for younger retirees as it allows much greater flexibility, particularly the capacity to reduce the level of income. This tranche can be reduced to £1,209 a year gross (35% of the maximum) if and when the consultancy income is received.

If the project is delayed, fails, lasts for a shorter period than expected or at a lower level of income than forecast, a further tranche of pension can be drawn from the remaining £400,000.

When full and formal retirement comes, the same mechanism could be adopted in larger proportions to generate tax-efficient income.

Portfolio review As Christopher's portfolio is largely inherited following his mother's death, it is high time for a review. It is likely that his mother had different investment objectives and, given the high rate of job turnover in the fund management industry, it is probable that some of these investments are no longer the best options.

However, before passing judgment on individual holdings, it is important to decide on an overall asset allocation strategy. Careful regard has to be given to the tax consequences and assets – whether inside the pension fund or in the portfolio – should be considered jointly to avoid unnecessary duplication with associated costs.

For a medium-risk balanced investor, a "model" strategy would be:
- 35% UK equities (smaller companies no more than 10%)
- 10% European equities
- 5% North American equities
- 5% Japan/Far East
- 30% fixed interest
- 15% property

When assessing which individual holdings should be sold and reinvested elsewhere, the portfolio should be considered jointly (even if Jane wants to keep her earnings to herself), as this will capitalise on tax efficiency. During this process, the model strategy could be adjusted to reflect Christopher and Jane's personal preferences.

Tax efficiency Before any changes are made to the portfolio, it should be split between Christopher and Jane so that any transactions will benefit from both of their capital gains tax allowances. The transfer of assets between spouses is free of CGT and the inherent liability is transferred to the new owner.

The income generating funds – the fixed-interest and UK bluechip elements of the portfolio and the savings accounts – are best held in Jane's name as she pays lower levels of income tax. If the overhaul of the portfolio turns out to be far reaching and does generate a CGT liability, this should be borne by Jane as she would pay at a lower level than Christopher. The CGT payment can also be deferred through investing in venture capital trusts, which should count against the UK smaller company component of the model portfolio.

Also, in the process of reorganising the portfolio any encashments that need to be reinvested should be done through a maxi equity Isa. The couple have £14,000 of tax-free Isa allowances which they can use each year. Should Christopher's high-paid consultancy project come off, the excess monies should be used to purchase further Isas. Otherwise, part of the portfolio should be sold within the CGT annual exemption limits each year and Isas bought with the proceeds. In this way, the portfolio will gradually move from being tax liable to tax-free.

The holdings split between Christopher and Jane could be:

Investment	Amount
Jane's portfolio	
Cash	£47,000
Tessa-only Isas	£9,000
Isas	£7,000
Unit/investment trusts	£62,000 or £53,000*
Christopher's portfolio	
Tessa-only Isas	£9,000
Peps	£30,000
Isas	£7,000
Unit/investment trusts	£62,000 or £53,000*
Pension	£444,544 or £464,000*
Total	**£677,544 or £679,000**

*depending on whether Christopher decides to live off his investments for the next nine months or start his pension drawdown.

Christopher should obtain a forecast of his state pension entitlements from age 65. This is achieved by filling in form BR19 available from DSS offices. This will show whether he needs to pay voluntary National Insurance contributions while he is not earning to maximise his state pension.

14

Planning for the fourth age

Investments that suit people in their late fifties or early sixties will not necessarily be appropriate for those entering the fourth age, in other words their mid seventies and eighties. Spending needs may suddenly jump if regular nursing or residential care is required, and people whose main pension has not been index-linked may start to feel the pinch, even if inflation, miraculously, stays at about 2% for the next 20 years.

In any case, there comes a time when some of the words that trip off a financial adviser's tongue – "long-term growth" for instance – seem rather less relevant than they were 20 years earlier. You may be more concerned these days with capital preservation than growth; you may welcome an increase in disposable income, and last, but by no means least, your thoughts may be turning to what you can give away now to children or grandchildren, rather than leaving it to be gobbled up by inheritance tax later on. This chapter looks at three main topics:

◆ Switching from growth to income investments
◆ Purchased life annuities
◆ How to get an income or capital sum from your home

The following chapter looks at steps you can take to minimise inheritance tax.

Switching from growth to income

Benjamin Franklin may have been right in saying that the only two certainties in life are death and taxes. Unfortunately, neither he nor anyone else can guarantee that tax regulations will remain unchanged. Inevitably, there will be some changes, but whether for good or bad we cannot know. Take the case of Isas and Peps. At present, basic rate taxpayers who hold Peps or Isas invested in bonds or cash deposits can reclaim the full 20% tax on the interest, but where the income comes from share dividends, only 10% tax can be reclaimed. In both cases, higher rate taxpayers are sheltered from all additional tax.

The government has said that this 10% reclaim on dividend income will remain in place only until 2004. It has said nothing at all about how long interest arising within a Pep or Isa will remain tax-free, nor about how long the other tax advantage of the schemes – their freedom from capital gains tax (CGT) – might last.

However, the likelihood has to be that even if Peps and Isas do not remain in exactly their current form, there will be a similar sort of scheme with similar tax concessions. Any wholesale removal of these concessions would provoke such an outcry that no sane government would attempt it. In the meantime, all we can do is plan on the basis of what is – and hope for the best.

If people have used their Pep and Isa allowances regularly in the past, this should mean that much, if not all, of their investment portfolio is held within these tax-free schemes. It certainly makes it easier to organise changes to investments which may now be appropriate. Outside Peps or Isas, you could face a significant CGT bill if you want to swap from equities to fixed-interest deposits; inside them, you can do so with no tax arising.

Timing

When is the time to make this switch? There is no sensible answer to this question, other than "it all depends". It depends on your income from other sources, on how much you need extra income and on how long you think you might live. But whenever you decide to do so, it is always wise to take your time over such a switch. This is especially so if you may face a CGT bill. By making use of your annual exemption and spreading your realisation of investments over several years, you may be able to eliminate CGT or at least reduce it considerably.

Even if your investments are all within the tax shelter of Peps and Isas, it makes sense to make changes over time. It is all about cutting down investment risk: selling out of the equity market at the wrong time is just as bad as buying at the wrong time. You can never know for certain when the best time is, but by staggering your switches, you can average out good and bad times.

So what do you switch to? It depends on the shape of your portfolio and your income needs. Some money, perhaps, can go into cash deposits, especially if by now you have no income tax liability. But if you are switching from an equity-invested Pep or Isa, another strong candidate must be a corporate bond fund. This could could double your immediate income, from (currently) about 3% to 6%.

Of course, the drawback with corporate bond income is that it is unlikely to rise in the future, unlike dividends from company shares. But there does come a time when the emphasis should be more on what you can get now, rather than the potential for growth.

Annuities

If you are not concerned about keeping access to your capital, another possibility is to buy an ordinary annuity, known as a purchased life annuity. Table 20 shows current rates for these for different ages. The older you are, the higher the income. Men receive more than women, because their life expectancy is lower.

The advantage of annuities is two-fold. First, as is evident from the table, you get a much higher income from these than is possible anywhere else – which is as it should be, given that you are exchanging the capital in return for a life-long income.

Table 20
Gross annual annuity payments for a purchase price of £10,000

Annuitant	Payment	Annuitant	Payment
Man 75	£1,166.49	Woman 75	£1,002.89
Man 80	£1,440.27	Woman 80	£1,224.00
Joint, both 75	£857.77		

Source: Hinton & Wild

The second advantage is revealed by table 21. This shows the amount of "capital content" of each payment. Purchased life annuities are taxed in a special way. A set amount of each payment counts as a return of original capital and this portion is tax-free. The older you are at the time you buy, the greater the proportion of each payment that is counted as capital. Only the balance is taxable so there is little tax to pay.

Table 21
Amount of tax-free content per year on payments produced by a £10,000 purchase price

Annuitant	Payment	Annuitant	Payment
Man 75	£911.59	Woman 75	£771.74
Man 80	£1,196.92	Woman 80	£1,026.76
Joint, both 75	£630.64		

Source: Hinton & Wild

Timing your annuity purchase is important. The payments you get are fixed at the outset and depend on long-term interest rates when you buy. At present, interest rates are much lower than they have been for a long time, so this is probably not the best time to buy – although that said, they may have further to fall. But as you are probably not contemplating an annuity purchase immediately, this is something to keep in the back of your mind. If, for example, in ten or 15 years, interest rates are much higher, but experts are predicting a fall, this would probably be a good time to buy.

Given that annuity payments are guaranteed for life, the longer you live the better the deal you get. This makes them especially good for people whose family has a record of collecting telegrams from the Queen, but not such a great choice for those that don't. If you do have health problems or are a smoker, consult an independent adviser – it is possible to get better annuity rates.

Annuities and inheritance tax planning

Annuities can have a role in inheritance tax planning. If your estate is valued at more than the nil-rate band, your heirs face a tax charge at 40%

on the excess. The current nil-rate band for inheritance tax (IHT) is £242,000 (2001-02 tax year) and if you own a house in the south of England, it may not take much, if anything, in the way of additional assets to hit that mark.

The best and simplest way to save IHT is to give away money seven years before you die, in which case, the gift becomes exempt. That is fine if you have the cash to spare but impossible if you need that cash to produce the income you live on. This is where an annuity could come in useful, as the following example shows.

Alfred Denny is a 75-year-old widower whose two nephews are his only relations. He lives in a mortgage-free house on modest occupational and state pensions plus the interest from capital saved in his building society, which totals £140,000. At current interest rates, this provides him with an extra £5,000 a year after basic rate tax. Both nephews are now at the property-buying stage and he would like to help them – but he cannot afford to give away much of his capital as he needs the extra income to live on. They are the principal beneficiaries in his will, but he would like to help them now, not after he is dead.

Denny spends £45,000 on a purchased life annuity, which guarantees a net income of almost exactly £5,000 a year for life, and gives them each £30,000 now to use as a deposit. As long as he lives for the next seven years, these gifts will be tax-free. If he left that sum to them on death – given that his property will use up the whole of the IHT nil-rate band – they would face an IHT bill of £24,000.

Other investments

Other investments for producing a higher income in old age are basically variations on this theme of turning some of your capital into income. For example, high coupon gilts (those with a high running yield), give you a good income now, but with the prospect of some capital loss when they mature.

Then there are the income shares of split-capital trusts, which, again, may provide a high income now but will probably lead to a capital loss when the trust winds up. These may be suitable if you are keen on managing your own investments, or they may play a part in a managed portfolio run by a stockbroker or investment adviser.

But what many people in their late seventies and eighties want above all is simplicity. By the time you reach 80-odd, you really can think about spending some of your capital. If you need persuading, just remember – it can save your heirs inheritance tax.

Using your home for income

Many people are, in terms of total assets, "rich", thanks to the value of their property yet find it hard to make ends meet. One possibility is to sell your house in exchange for a smaller and cheaper one, thus realising your capital.

But if you want to carry on living in the same house, there are alternatives. You can sell it – or part of it – to someone else, while retaining the right to live there for the rest of your life. Or you can raise a mortgage on it, where the interest is rolled up until death – so you have nothing to pay and, once again, have a capital sum in your hands. Both types of scheme have drawbacks as well as benefits.

Home reversion schemes

These involve selling all or a portion of your property to a financial institution in return for a capital sum or a guaranteed income for life (or perhaps a mixture of the two). The price you get depends largely on how old you are, but it will always be a great deal less than the property's open market value. The older you are, the more you get and, following a pattern which is probably familiar by now, single men get more than single women of the same age, thanks to their lower life expectancy. But even if a single man delayed taking out such a plan until age 80, for example, he would, at most, get only a little over half the current market value.

Table 22 shows examples of what schemes currently provide at various ages. Most are open to people over 65, but if you can afford to wait, you will get a better deal.

Table 22
Home reversion schemes: amount of capital or income available assuming a freehold property is worth £100,000 and the owner sells three-quarters

Cash

Age	Woman	Man	Age	Couple
70	£33,815	£36,693	Both 70	£30,119
75	£37,515	£40,089	Both 75	£34,630
80	£41,433	£43,476	Both 80	£38,257

Or annual income for life

Age	Woman	Man	Age	Couple
70	£2,787	£3,761	Both 70	£1,979
75	£3,919	£5,177	Both 75	£2,842
80	£5,349	£6,851	Both 80	£4,073

Note: income shown is net of basic rate tax. Non-taxpayers would receive slightly higher benefits

Source: Hinton & Wild

Equity-release mortgages

Several companies offer fixed-rate mortgages to retired people where interest is charged but rolled up and not repayable until after death. This means they can realise a cash sum and not worry about interest payments. All the schemes currently available incorporate a guarantee that the total of the loan plus interest will not exceed the value of your property on death – which means you will not leave your heirs a hefty interest bill.

The maximum loan available depends on your age and, once again, your sex. The older you are at the outset, the higher it will be. It is likely to be around 20% of the current value of the property at age 60, rising to a maximum of 50% at 89. The schemes are available from 60 or 65 upwards.

You can take out a smaller loan than the maximum at an early age and come back for more in five or ten years, rather than take the whole lot at once – this will help cut down the interest bill.

Which type of scheme is best?

There is no simple answer. There is one big difference between the schemes. With home reversion, if you sell only a portion of your property outright, the rest remains yours and its increasing value will eventually benefit your heirs. The longer you live, the greater this remaining value is likely to be, assuming house prices continue rising. With an equity release mortgage, the longer you live, the more the rolled up interest will amount to and the greater the likelihood that there will be nothing left over for heirs once the interest bill has been met.

One important factor with both schemes is whether the extra income or capital sum would affect your eligibility for various state benefits such as income support. The Citizens' Advice Bureau may be able to advise on this. Both schemes can cut the inheritance tax due after your death.

Where to get more information and advice

The charity Age Concern publishes a booklet on these schemes entitled *Using Your Home as Capital*, which I thoroughly recommend if you or a relative are considering such a move. Age Concern also has a factsheet – number 12, *Raising Income or Capital from Your Home* – which is available free to retired people. You can get a copy by calling its information line on 0800 009966 or view it on the website at www.ageconcern.org.uk

Most of the companies offering these schemes are members of an organisation called Ship – Safe Home Income Plans – which also publishes some information on them. It operates a code of conduct which insists, for example, that no member can arrange a plan unless a client's solicitor has signed a certificate stating that he or she has explained the scheme and believes the client fully understands the benefits and obligations.

Other ways of making your home pay

You might consider letting a room on a permanent or occasional basis. In either case, you should be able to benefit from "rent-a-room" tax relief, which allows income of up to £4,250 tax-free. If you expect the rent to come to more than this, it is worth consulting an accountant to establish whether rent-a-room is preferable to a normal letting arrangement, which would allow you to claim against tax certain expenses involved in letting – with rent-a-room, no expenses are allowable.

15

Making a will

It is estimated that over half the adults in the UK have not got around to making a will. Retirement is an excellent time to put the matter right. If you die without making a valid will, your estate is divided up according to the intestacy rules. These rules aim to be fair to all potential beneficiaries, but it is highly unlikely that they would mirror your own wishes. Even if they did, having a valid will should make clearing up your estate quicker and simpler. This chapter covers:

- Intestacy rules in England and Wales
- Intestacy rules in Scotland
- How to make a will
- Choosing executors
- Deeds of family arrangement

The need to review an existing will

Even if you have made a will in the past, once you have retired you may well need to review and possibly rewrite it. Before retirement, for example, you may have significant life assurance benefits under your pension plan but after retirement, this cover lapses, so you may need to rearrange the disposal of your other assets. In England and Wales (but not Scotland) getting married automatically revokes any will you made previously, unless it expressly states that it was made in contemplation of marriage.

The intestacy rules in England and Wales

The full rules run to around half-a-dozen closely printed pages, but the basics are as follows. They are also summarised in the chart opposite.

- **If you are married with children** Your spouse gets your personal belongings, the first £125,000 absolutely and a "life interest" (the income but not the capital) in half the rest. The children, assuming they survive to age 18, get the balance in equal shares and the remainder of the estate when your spouse dies. If your children die before you, their children step up into their shoes.
- **If you are married without children** Your spouse gets the personal belongings, the first £200,000 absolutely and half the balance absolutely. The rest goes to relatives in a pecking order which starts with your parents. If they are dead, it goes to your brothers and sisters or, if they are dead, to their children – your nephews and nieces – and, if they are dead, to their children, and so on. If your parents are dead and you have no brothers or sisters, your spouse receives everything absolutely.
- **If you are single** The estate goes to your children. If you have none, it goes to your parents. If they are dead, it goes to your brothers or sisters or, if they are dead, to their children. If you have no brothers or sisters, it goes to your grandparents, if alive; if not, to uncles or aunts (or their children or grandchildren). If you have no living relatives within these definitions, the whole estate goes to the Crown.
- **If you are living with someone, but not married** Your partner has no rights under the intestacy laws, no matter how long you might have lived together. However, under the Inheritance Act, partners have similar rights to spouses, as long as they have lived with their partner as common-law man or wife for at least two years before death.

While, in England and Wales, there are few rules about who you must leave your money to, the law does try to ensure that families and dependants are adequately catered for. If a widow or an unmarried former wife, who was dependent on you immediately before your death, is cut out of your will or left an inadequate amount, she is entitled to go to the courts and to ask for more. Dependants is defined very widely and may include, for example, a godchild for whose education you were paying.

Making a will

ARE YOU MARRIED?

YES branch:

IS YOUR ESTATE WORTH MORE THAN £125,000?

- **NO** → EVERYTHING GOES TO SPOUSE*
- **YES** → **DO YOU HAVE CHILDREN?**
  - **YES** → SPOUSE GETS PERSONAL EFFECTS, FIRST £125,000* AND A LIFE INTEREST IN HALF THE REMAINDER. CHILDREN OR THEIR ISSUE GET THE REST
  - **NO** → **DO YOU HAVE PARENTS?**
    - **YES** → SPOUSE GETS PERSONAL EFFECTS, FIRST £200,000* PLUS HALF THE REMAINDER. PARENTS GET THE REST
    - **NO** → **DO YOU HAVE BROTHERS OR SISTERS?**
      - **YES** → SPOUSE GETS PERSONAL EFFECTS, FIRST £200,000* PLUS HALF THE REMAINDER. BROTHERS AND SISTERS OR THEIR ISSUE GET THE REST
      - **NO** → EVERYTHING GOES TO SPOUSE*

NO branch:

DO YOU HAVE CHILDREN?

- **YES** → SHARED EQUALLY BETWEEN THEM OR THEIR ISSUE
- **NO** → **DO YOU HAVE PARENTS?**
  - **YES** → SHARED EQUALLY BETWEEN THEM
  - **NO** → **DO YOU HAVE BROTHERS OR SISTERS?**
    - **YES** → SHARED EQUALLY BETWEEN THEM OR THEIR ISSUE
    - **NO** → **DO YOU HAVE GRANDPARENTS?**
      - **YES** → SHARED EQUALLY BETWEEN THEM
      - **NO** → **DO YOU HAVE UNCLES AND AUNTS?**
        - **YES** → SHARED EQUALLY BETWEEN THEM OR THEIR ISSUE
        - **NO** → EVERYTHING GOES TO THE CROWN

---

* The spouse will benefit only if he or she survives the intestate by 28 days. Where the spouse does not survive, the intestate estate will be dealt with as if there had been no spouse.

Issue means children (including illegitimate and adopted), grandchildren, great grandchildren, etc.

Brothers and sisters of whole blood come before brothers and sisters of half blood. Uncles and aunts of whole blood come before uncles and aunts of half blood.

The intestacy rules in Scotland

In Scotland, if you leave a widow or widower, there is a distinction between "prior rights" and "legal rights". Getting married or divorced does not make any previous will invalid. The Inheritance Act does not apply to Scotland. The following is an outline of the situation:

- **Prior rights** If you are married when you die, your surviving spouse is entitled to the first £130,000 worth of the family home and the first £22,000 of fixtures and fittings. If you have no children, your spouse is also entitled to the first £58,000 of other assets. If you have children, this right is restricted to the first £35,000 of other assets.
- **Legal rights** These apply whether or not you have made a will. You cannot completely disinherit your spouse or children. If you have no children, your spouse is entitled to half of your moveable estate, irrespective of the terms of the will. Moveable estate is everything except land and buildings.

    If you have children but no spouse, they are entitled to half of the moveable estate between them. If both children and spouse survive you, your spouse's legal rights are one-third of the moveable estate and your children's are also one-third, shared between them. Your spouse or any of your children can make this claim. If none is made, the estate will be divided in accordance with any will you leave.
- **Marriage and living together** In Scotland it is possible to be declared married by the courts if you have lived together as man and wife and were both free to marry. This is known as marriage by habit and repute and needs to be established by the court. Evidence would include, for example, sharing the same surname, being known as Mr and Mrs by family and friends, and having those names on the bills and the electoral register. If you live together but are not known as Mr and Mrs, your partner has no rights of inheritance unless you leave a will.
- **If you are single without children** The estate passes to your siblings or their children; if none, to parents or grandparents and, if none, to great uncles and aunts and their descendants, until some relative is found to inherit. If there are none, it goes to the Crown.

The intestacy rules in Northern Ireland

The rules in Northern Ireland are similar to those in England and Wales but not identical. No life interest is created in Northern Ireland and the pecking order of relatives who inherit is slightly different.

How to make a will

You can do this yourself, use a will-writing agency or go to a solicitor. The DIY route is cheapest, involving no more than a few pounds for a special kit. Given the difference in the law, it is vital that people living in Scotland do not use forms designed for England and Wales or vice versa.

There are a number of specialist will-writing agencies, some set up by insurance companies, others run by charities. You might want to read up further before embarking on your will: see Age Concern's factsheet, available on its website at www.ageconcern.org.uk for England and Wales or by calling 0800 00 9966. Ask for factsheet 7S for Scotland.

Going to a solicitor is the most obvious choice and probably the most sensible for most people. The cost will vary widely, mainly according to the amount of time he or she has to spend, so make sure you know what you want to say, otherwise you will end up wasting time and money.

Wording your will

The usual form of will is to choose one or more people as the main beneficiaries of the residue of your estate after any gifts have been made. It may also include gifts to individuals or charities – either sums of money or items such as jewellery, which should be described clearly so there is no doubt what you mean. Shakespeare, you may remember, left Anne Hathaway his "second-best bed" – if you follow his example, you had better make sure it is clear which one is second best.

Before you get carried away, remember that if your total estate, including your house, comes to more than the nil-rate band for IHT (£242,000 in the 2001-02 tax year) there will be tax to pay at 40% on the balance. Do not leave so much in specific bequests that your main beneficiary does not have enough once these and the tax have been paid.

Appointing executors

Executors are the people named in the will to deal with your affairs. Most people appoint a relative and it is probably best to appoint two (for instance, your spouse and a brother or sister) in case one dies before you or simply to share the burden. Executors can be beneficiaries.

It is also possible to appoint a professional executor, such as a solicitor, accountant or banker, though this will involve a charge usually paid out of your estate. It may be better to keep your relatives as executors, leaving it to them to call in professional help if they need it.

Signing the will and storing it

You need two people to witness your signature; but they do not need to see the will's contents to do so. They must not benefit under it, nor must their spouses. You must then decide where to keep it - you can store it with your bank or solicitor, for example, keeping a copy yourself.

Revising the will

As mentioned earlier, in England and Wales (but not in Scotland) a will becomes invalid if you marry or remarry, unless it is expressly made in contemplation of marriage to a named person, so you will need to make a new one at this point. Otherwise, minor variations can be achieved by adding a codicil (supplement) which must itself be witnessed - they do not need to be the same witnesses as for the original. But if the changes are substantial, it is best to start afresh.

Making it easy for your executors

Making matters easy for your executors also means making matters easy for yourself in the meantime. If your idea of financial planning is to throw everything into a shoebox, you will no doubt find the annual task of filling in your tax return a nightmare. You could also be losing money - for instance, by keeping money in old accounts paying little interest.

Now that you are about to retire, make a resolution to spend at least a day or two setting up a clear filing system, with a summary of your investments and savings which you can give to your executors, telling them at the same time where your will and other documents are stored.

Deeds of variation

A will is not necessarily the final word on the matter of how your assets are distributed. It is possible for a "deed of variation" to be executed after your death which alters the distribution. The deed must be signed by all those beneficiaries under the will who will be disadvantaged by the new arrangement - in practice, it is often signed by all beneficiaries, including those who benefit from the variation - and it must be completed within two years of your death. One of the most common reasons for using such a deed is to avoid or reduce inheritance tax.

16

Inheritance tax planning

At some point, our thoughts turn to how we can help the generations coming after us and, equally, how to ensure that our savings are not grabbed by the taxman after we die. Handing over a large slice of our money to government coffers might count as one way of helping society, but most people would rather benefit their family, friends or particular charities. This chapter looks at:

- How inheritance tax works
- How to calculate your IHT liability
- Planning to reduce your liability
- Lifetime gifts and other measures

How inheritance tax works

Inheritance tax (IHT) is potentially payable on gifts made during your life and on assets passing at death. The main exemption is for assets passing between husband and wife, whether during life or at death.

If you give away assets to anyone other than your spouse during your lifetime, these do not immediately attract tax. Depending on how much they are, and to whom they are made, they may be fully exempt from the start or "potentially exempt". If they are potentially exempt, as long as you live seven years after making the gift, they become fully exempt and no tax will be due on them. If not, they will fall within the tax net.

Everyone is entitled to give away a certain amount of assets free from

IHT – or, technically, with the tax chargeable at a nil rate. The amount of this nil-rate band rises each year, usually in line with inflation. In 2001-02 it is £242,000. Assets above this limit attract tax at a flat rate of 40%.

How to calculate your liability

IHT is often, and quite inaccurately, labelled a rich man's tax. The value of many people's home will use up the nil-rate band, which means that IHT could be payable on the rest of their estate. All investments fall into the melting pot, including Peps, Tessas and Isas. These may have been tax-free during life but they are not immune from IHT on death. The one saving grace is that no capital gains tax is payable on death.

To work out how much could be due on your death, add up the current value of everything you own. If you decide to leave all your assets to your husband or wife, no IHT is payable. If you are single, the whole value of your estate, less the nil-rate band, may be subject to IHT at 40%, although any money left to charity or to a political party is exempt.

Planning to reduce IHT

The key to escaping inheritance tax is to die with nothing, having given it all away before – which is easier said than done. Less dramatically, it is worth getting to know the rules, so you can ensure that whatever you give away during your life is given in the most tax-efficient way.

Lifetime gifts

Certain gifts made during your lifetime are immediately exempt from the tax. The rest are not. Once you reach a certain age, you should bear in mind that you will need to live for the next seven years for any potentially exempt gift to escape fully from the tax. You should keep a record of such gifts and when they were made.

Immediately exempt gifts

- Up to £3,000 per year, to anyone. If unused, this allowance can be carried forward, but only for one year, and the current year's allowance must be used up first.
- Gifts of no more than £250 each to as many people as you like each year. But if a recipient gets more than this sum from you in a year, you cannot claim exemption on the first £250.
- Regular gifts which form "part of your normal expenditure out of income". This is not strictly defined in the legislation, but it means the

gifts must come from your income, not your capital, and should not be so great as to diminish your usual standard of living.
◆ Gifts made on marriage. Parents are allowed to give £5,000 to each of their children (each parent has this allowance). Grandparents can give £2,500 each and any other relative or friend can give £1,000.
◆ Gifts of any amount made from husband to wife or vice versa, as long as both are domiciled in this country. If your spouse is not, the maximum exempt gift is £55,000.
◆ Gifts of any amount to charities, to recognised political parties and to certain institutions such as the British Museum.
◆ Gifts for the maintenance of your family including, for example, to children under 18 or still in full-time education.

Any other gifts you make during your lifetime are potentially exempt transfers. When you die, the value of all such gifts made within the previous seven years is added up and set against the nil-rate band. If the total of these lifetime gifts exceeds the nil-rate band, there is some taper relief available on the excess, depending on how long you lived after making the gift – table 23 gives details.

Table 23
Taper relief on lifetime gifts

Years between gift and death	% of full IHT rate payable
0-3	100%
3-4	80%
4-5	60%
5-6	40%
6-7	20%

Suppose you had made a potentially exempt gift of £10,000 (having already used up your nil-rate band with previous gifts) and died just over four years later. The tax payable on this gift would be £2,400 because it would be paid at the rate of 60% of 40% – in other words, at 24%.

In practice, taper relief is rarely used. Most people do not give such big gifts during their lifetimes as would use up the nil-rate band and more.

Gifts with reservation

Gifts made during your lifetime have to be genuine. The Inland Revenue has a special category of "gifts with reservation" – where you pretend to give something away but keep rights over it. For example, if you "give" your home to your children but retain the right to live in it without paying a commercial rent, as far as it is concerned, this is not a gift at all.

Using your nil-rate band on death

IHT may not seem an immediate problem to couples, as the first to die would usually leave everything to their spouse and no IHT is payable on assets passed to a husband or wife. But you should plan ahead so that at least part of your nil-rate band is used, even if you are the first to die. The following example shows why this is important.

John Walker decides to leave his share of his home (worth £350,000 in total) to his wife Anne, together with its contents. His company pension falls to two-thirds on his death, so he leaves most of his savings, totalling £200,000, to her as well. He leaves £5,000 each to his two children and £5,000 to an old friend. Result: no tax is payable as everything left to his wife is free of IHT and his other bequests are well within the nil-rate band.

Anne dies two years later. Her estate is now worth £600,000, as the house has increased in value. She leaves it in equal shares to her children. Result: the first £242,000 falls in the nil-rate band, but the balance – £358,000 – is liable to IHT at 40%, making a total bill of £143,200.

If John had left each of his children £50,000 rather than £5,000, there would still have been no IHT to pay on his death and the IHT payable on Anne's death would (assuming no rise in the nil-rate band in the meantime) be only £107,200, a saving of £36,000.

Thinking further ahead, you should consider leaving at least some money to grandchildren rather than children, as this way you skip one generation's worth of IHT.

Life assurance

This is not so much a way of reducing IHT as ensuring that your heirs have the means to pay it. If you take out a regular premium life assurance policy for the benefit of your children, the premiums will normally count as exempt lifetime gifts, because they are regular and are paid out of your income. The policy can be written in trust so that its proceeds, payable on your death, are free from IHT. For married couples, the policy can be a joint one, which pays out on the second death (as this is likely to be when the bulk of the IHT is due).

In theory, the amount the policy guarantees to pay out on death should be 40% of the value of your assets (less the nil-rate band) to meet the IHT bill in full. In practice, there's no reason why it should not be less – every little helps. Get professional advice on what sort of policy to buy and what type of trust to use.

IHT and your home

One of the biggest problems with IHT planning is your home. It is the main reason so many otherwise modest estates fall within the tax net, but there is no simple means of escape. As mentioned above, if you give away your home during your life but keep the right to live there, this does not count as a gift, unless you pay a full commercial rent.

One possibility is to change the form of ownership under which you hold the property. Most couples own their home under a joint tenancy, where one person's half passes automatically to the other on death. It is also possible to hold it as tenants in common, which means each person owns a separate 50% share, which they can pass as they wish on death. You could bequeath half of your half share to your children. Your widow or widower would still have the undisputed right to live there for the rest of their life, but it would also mean that at least part of the nil-rate band would be used on the first death.

You need to think carefully before embarking on such a scheme. It is possible, if unlikely, that relations with your children might deteriorate after the first death. Another snag is that the subsequent divorce of one of your children could mean their share of the property was counted in any divorce settlement. Practical problems might also arise if the survivor wanted to sell up and move somewhere else.

IHT and trusts

There are a number of ways in which assets can be put into trust for the benefit of future generations, bypassing or at least minimising IHT. This is a highly complex area and one which the Revenue has shown a propensity to attack. If you are interested in setting up a trust, you will need ongoing professional advice to ensure that it remains a successful way of avoiding IHT.

IHT-friendly investments

The problem with most IHT planning is that we cannot afford to give away our assets during lifetime, because we need the income they produce.

There are some types of investment which can be useful in this respect, such as an annuity. You give up a capital sum in return for a guaranteed lifetime income so there is less capital to leave to your heirs, but, at the same time, less tax to pay. The following example shows how this might work.

Janet Jones is 75. Her house is worth £242,000 – the same amount as the IHT nil-rate band. She has a small pension and deposits in a building society of £100,000, giving her an income of £4,500 a year gross, which she needs to live on. On her death, her two children, who will inherit the house and the savings, will have to pay inheritance tax of £40,000 (40% of £100,000 – assuming its value continues to match the nil-rate band).

Instead, she buys an annuity with £50,000 which gives her a guaranteed gross income of £5,000. She gives £20,000 to each of her children, leaving her with £10,000 in her building society. On her death at age 83, her children face an inheritance tax bill of just £4,000 (40% of £10,000) – a saving of £36,000. The children have benefited by getting the money a great deal earlier – if they invested it in a building society account earning interest at 4.5% until the time of her death, they would have £32,708 each. Meanwhile, their mother has had the pleasure of giving it away – and enjoyed a slightly higher income.

IHT: the last word

No-one likes paying tax, but it is important to keep a sense of perspective. It is far more important for your widow or widower to have enough to manage on comfortably than to use the whole of your nil-rate band gifting assets to children or grandchildren.

A little bit of planning – using the £3,000 annual exemption, for example, or making regular gifts out of income – will certainly save some tax and for many people, there will be little need to go any further.

17

Planning for income and capital gains tax

Sometimes people seem more concerned about inheritance tax – which is payable only after they have died – than they are about income tax and capital gains tax, payable while they are still very much alive. This is understandable in a sense as IHT can prove very costly, while the depredations of income and capital gains tax are generally much smaller.

This chapter looks at the main aspects of these two taxes as they are likely to impinge on your life after retirement and, in particular, at:

- ◆ Personal allowances
- ◆ The age allowance trap
- ◆ Tax on investments
- ◆ Capital gains tax
- ◆ The self-assessment timetable

Bear in mind that this is not a tax textbook and if you want more detailed information, you should look elsewhere. The Inland Revenue website at www.inlandrevenue.gov.uk probably contains all the information you require and more – but some of the booklets reproduced on the site may not be completely up to date and you will need to make further checks if there has been a recent announcement of changes.

You can also get information from your local tax office – listed in the telephone book under Inland Revenue – or you can call its information centre on 020 7667 4001. There is also a self-assessment helpline on 0845 9000 444.

If you want information on a specific point but have no wish to go into personal details, you are not alone. It is very common for tax offices to receive enquiries starting: "I have a friend who…"

Income tax: personal allowances

Everyone has the right to a certain level of income free of tax. These personal allowances are set at a higher level once the taxpayer reaches 65 and there is a further increase at age 75. The state pension, which is always paid gross, may use up the lion's share of the personal allowance. Thereafter, income is taxed at a rate which rises from 10% for the first slice of taxable income to a maximum of 40%. The rate depends partly on the type of income – whether it counts as earned (a category that includes all pensions) or investment income – full details are given below. The personal allowance levels and tax rates for the 2001-02 tax year are shown at the end of this chapter.

The age allowance trap

Everyone over the age of 65 is entitled to the higher age allowance. If you are married and one of you was born before 6 April, 1935, there is an extra married couple's allowance. But these allowances will be withdrawn if your income in a tax year exceeds £17,600. It is withdrawn at the rate of £1 for every £2 of extra income, until you are back with the ordinary, under-65 level. Once this has gone, the extra married couple's allowance, if you have it, is whittled away at the same rate until it no longer exists.

The effect of this withdrawal is to make your "marginal rate" (the rate you pay on the top slice of your income) somewhere between 27% and 33%, depending on whether you are entitled to the married couple's allowance and on whether your income comes from pensions or investments.

Broadly speaking, if you have income of more than about £27,000, all your age allowances will have been whittled away.

If your income is somewhere between these two levels, there may be steps you can take to limit the effect of the trap:
- ◆ If you are married, you might consider giving investments to your partner, if they have a lower income, so that the income they provide will be counted as theirs. Note: you cannot give any of your pension income to your partner – it is always taxed as if it belongs to you.

◆ You can change the type of investments you hold. Interest from cash Isas and National Savings certificates is tax-free and will not count for age allowance purposes. Nor will income produced by equity Isas or Peps. You are allowed to withdraw up to 5% a year from single premium life assurance bonds, including with-profits bonds, for a period of up to 20 years without any immediate tax liability. These withdrawals are treated as a return of your capital so, once again, are tax-free and will not affect your age allowance.

No sensible adviser would suggest you invest in something purely because it would help to preserve your age allowance. But if you are deciding between two investments, both of which are equally suitable for you, this point could help you choose.

Income tax: planning pre-retirement

Employees who are within a year or so of retirement should make a mental note to look at their tax affairs as they enter their last tax year in employment. If you are retiring part way through a tax year, it is a good idea to write to your Inspector of Taxes a few months earlier asking for your coding to be amended from the date of retirement. Your income will change from the date of retirement and you may also be without a host of taxable benefits such as a company car, private medical insurance and so on. These can usually be apportioned so that if, for example, you give them up half way through the year, you pay only half the tax and your tax code should be increased.

How income is taxed

The basic rule is that earned income – which includes all types of pension – is taxed first and investment income comes second. Your marginal rate of tax applies to the top slice of your income and this will be the income that comes from your investments.

Pension income

As mentioned above, pensions from the state are paid gross but they are taxable. This applies to the basic pension, any graduated pension and any Serps entitlement. Other pension income, whether from a company or a personal pension, is usually paid net of basic rate tax, currently 22%. This can be reclaimed in full by non-taxpayers and those whose marginal rate is 10% can reclaim part of the tax. If your pension income lifts you above the level at which higher rate tax starts, you must pay an extra 18% of the gross.

Interest from banks and building societies

This will normally be paid net of 20% tax and basic rate taxpayers have no further liability. If you are a non-taxpayer, you can get the interest gross by filling out form R85, available from bank and building society branches or tax offices. If you have not done this before but were eligible to do so, you can reclaim the tax for up to six tax years from the time you make the claim.

Higher rate taxpayers must declare the gross interest received and will have to pay an extra of 20%. Those with a 10% marginal tax rate can reclaim the difference between 10% and 20% via their tax office.

Dividends from shares and unit trusts

Dividends are paid net of a notional 10% tax charge. The basic rate taxpayer has no further liability. Non-taxpayers and 10% taxpayers cannot reclaim this tax. Higher rate taxpayer must pay extra, equivalent to a total tax charge of 32.5% on the grossed up dividend.

Income withdrawals from life assurance bonds

The first 5% a year is treated as return of capital and is tax-free for a period of up to 20 years. Any higher amounts are free of tax for basic rate taxpayers but there is an extra charge for higher rate payers. Non-taxpayers cannot reclaim any tax.

Payments from purchased life annuities

Part of each payment counts as return of capital and is tax free. The proportion depends on your age at the time you bought the annuity. The balance is paid net of 20% tax which can be reclaimed by non-taxpayers. Higher rate taxpayers must pay extra.

Gifts of investments between husband and wife

The Revenue accepts that couples may swap assets to gain the maximum tax advantage, but such a rearrangement must be a genuine gift with no strings attached. Where assets are held jointly, it will treat the ownership as 50:50, unless you tell it otherwise.

Capital gains tax

Capital gains tax is payable on profits made on the sale or gift of any asset, although not on gifts between husbands and wives. Every taxpayer has an annual exempt allowance – £7,500 for the 2001-02 tax year – which normally rises in line with inflation. If you realise capital gains and losses in the same year, the one may be offset against the other to reduce the total.

Once gains exceed the annual allowance, they are potentially taxable as if they formed the top slice of your income – which means they may be taxed at 10%, 20% or 40%.

Almost everything you sell at a profit may be subject to CGT but there are some exceptions, the main one being your home. A fuller list is given at the end of this section.

CGT reliefs: indexation and tapering

Until April 1998, indexation relief applied to all assets, with the aim of ensuring that only "real" (ie after-inflation) gains were taxable. If you are selling assets now which you bought before April 1998, you can still make use of this relief, up to that date.

Under indexation relief, the original price of the asset is indexed up by the amount of inflation since purchase (using the March 1982 price in cases where assets have been held for longer) until April 1998. The taxable profit becomes the sale price less the inflated purchase price. To this you can add the costs of purchase (indexed in the same way) and the cost of the sale. Your local tax office can supply a table showing the correct indexation figures to apply.

In April 1998 a new system of taper relief was brought in, which reduces the percentage of the gain chargeable to tax depending on how long you have held the asset. If you are selling something you bought before April 1998 you will have to work with both systems, using indexation up to that date and taper relief thereafter.

How taper relief works

The idea behind taper relief is to encourage people to invest long term by reducing the chargeable gain the longer you hold an asset. If you sell something after you have held it for three to four complete years, only 95% of the gain is taxable, falling in stages to 60% if you have held it for ten complete years before selling. The table is at the end of the section.

CGT and tax planning

There is no doubt that CGT is complicated – it may be one of the few taxes where the prospect of calculating it, especially if you have built up your investments through a regular savings scheme, is even more daunting than the thought of paying it.

The following suggestions should help you avoid the first as well as the second:

◆ Use your tax-exempt annual allowance each year wherever possible. If you are reorganising your portfolio, try to spread this process over as many tax years as possible, to make use of two or more annual allowances.

◆ If you are married, remember that you are both entitled to an annual exempt allowance. Use these to the full by gifting assets to your spouse before they are sold. Gifts between husband and wife do not give rise to any immediate CGT liability. Instead, they "inherit" the purchase price and date of purchase from you. This is also worth doing if your partner has a lower income, as the rate at which they have to pay any CGT may be lower than yours. Note that gifts to any other members of your family, or anyone else, count as a disposal for CGT purposes and you may have to pay tax on them.

◆ If you are reinvesting the proceeds in some other investment, make use of your annual Isa allowance (currently £7,000). This will shelter them from CGT in the future.

◆ If you keep your total annual disposals to within twice the exempt allowance – in other words, to £15,000 in the 2001-02 tax year – and the taxable profit on these disposals is within the £7,500 allowance, you will not need to declare the disposals on your tax return.

◆ If you are happy to keep all your investments long term, remember that there is no CGT charge on death – this is where inheritance tax kicks in instead.

No more bed and breakfasting

It is no longer possible to escape CGT by using the "bed and breakfast" technique. This involved selling the shares one day and buying them back the next, using your annual allowance to establish a new, higher purchase price. This procedure was outlawed a few years ago. But you can still use the annual allowance for selling one lot of investments and buying something else. Or, if you are very organised, you can swap shares with your spouse in a bed and breakfast deal. You, for example, can sell your holding in XYZ Plc and buy shares in ABC Plc, while your partner sells their ABC shares and buys into XYZ.

All this, of course, has been rather theoretical over the last couple of years. It is more likely that investors have been suffering losses on their investments in recent times rather than enjoying gains. But one day, inevitably, the tide will turn and profits (and CGT) will become a reality once more.

Tax facts and figures for 2001-02

Income tax: personal allowances

Personal allowance (basic)	£4,535
Personal allowance (age 65-74)	£5,990
Personal allowance (age 75 & over)	£6,260
Married couple's allowance (age 65-74)*	£5,365
Married couple's allowance (age 75 & over)*	£5,435
Married couple's allowance (minimum amount)*	£2,070
Income limit for age-related allowances	£17,600
Blind person's allowance	£1,450
Rent-a-room tax-free income	£4,250

*Relief is restricted to 10%. Available only where at least one partner was born before 6 April, 1935.

Tax on earned income

Rate	Taxable income
10% on	first £1,880
22% on	next £27,520
40% on	the balance

Savings income

◆ **Interest** Taxpayers below the 40% threshold pay 20% on interest. Taxpayers whose marginal rate is 10% can reclaim 10%.

◆ **Dividends** Share dividends are paid net of a 10% tax credit which satisfies basic rate taxpayers' liability in full. Non-taxpayers and 10% taxpayers cannot reclaim the tax, while 40% taxpayers must pay extra, equivalent to a total charge of 32.5%.

Capital gains tax

Tax rate
The rate at which capital gains tax is paid on chargeable gains depends on your taxable income for the year. The gains are added to your income. If the total is:
- Below the basic rate (22%) starting limit, you are charged at 10%.
- Between the basic rate starting and top limits, you are charged at 20%.
- Above the higher rate (40%) starting limit, you are charged at 40%.

Annual exemptions
Personal   £7,500
Trusts   £3,750

Tax-free gains
There is no capital gains tax payable on gains made on the following:
- Your principal private residence
- Private cars
- Personal belongings (known as chattels – such as paintings or furniture) if sold for £6,000 or less
- Foreign currency bought for personal spending abroad
- British government stock, known as gilts
- Peps, Isas, National Savings certificates, most pension plans
- Shares in qualifying venture capital trusts, enterprise investment schemes and business expansion scheme shares bought after 18 March, 1986

Taxable gains
Indexation relief is available on assets bought on or before 5 April, 1998. Taper relief may be available on assets sold after April 1998. The percentage of the gain that is taxable is based on the number of complete years an asset is owned after 5 April, 1998.

Planning for income and capital gains tax

Years owned* after 5 April, 1998	% of gain that is taxable
1	100%
2	100%
3	95%
4	90%
5	85%
6	80%
7	75%
8	70%
9	65%
10	60%

*Assets held before 17 March, 1998 qualify for one year's extra taper relief.

Stamp duty

Stocks and marketable securities

The stamp duty rate is 0.5%.

Property

Value	Rate
Up to £60,000	Nil
£60,001–£250,000	1%
£250,001–£500,000	3%
£500,001+	4%

Properties in certain areas which are deemed to be "deprived" are free of stamp duty up to a purchase price of £150,000.

Main deadline dates for self-assessment

Filing tax returns

◆ **30 September** Deadline for filing completed tax return for previous year, if you want the Inland Revenue to calculate your tax for you.
◆ **30 September** Deadline for filing completed tax return for previous year if you want any tax you owe (up to £1,000) included in next year's tax code (applies to employees only).

- **5 October** Deadline for letting the Inland Revenue know if you need a tax return for previous year and have not been sent one.
- **31 January** Deadline for returning completed tax return for previous year, if you make the tax calculation yourself.

Fine for late filing: £100.
Additional fine if return not received by following 31 July: £100.

Paying tax

- **31 January** In current tax year: 50% of previous year's income tax, less tax deducted at source.
- **Following 31 July** 50% of income tax, less tax deducted at source.
- **Following 31 January** Balancing payment of income tax and all capital gains tax.

Fines for late payment

Currently 6.5% interest from due date.
Plus surcharges on balancing payment as follows:
- **28 February** If payment still not received, a 5% surcharge on any amount outstanding.
- **31 July** If payment still not received, a further 5% surcharge on any amount outstanding.

Useful names, addresses and websites

Regulation

Financial Services Authority
25 The North Colonnade
Canary Wharf
London E14 5HS
Tel: 0845 606 1234
Website: www.fsa.gov.uk
Consumer helpline email: consumerhelp@fsa.gov.uk

Ombudsmen

Financial Ombudsman Service
South Quay Plaza
183 Marsh Wall
London E14 9SR
Tel: 0845 080 1800
Website: www.financial-ombudsman.org.uk
For complaints about individual pensions and free-standing AVCs, life assurance, general insurance and investment products.

The Pensions Ombudsman
11 Belgrave Road
London SW1V 1RB
Tel: 020 7834 9144
Website: www.pensions-ombudsman.org.uk
For complaints about occupational pensions.

Office for the Supervision of Solicitors
Victoria Court
8 Dormer Place
Leamington Spa
Warks CV32 5AE
Tel: 01926 822007

Ombudsman for Estate Agents
Beckett House
4 Bridge Street
Salisbury
Wilts SP1 2LX
Tel: 01722 333306

Pensions

The Office for the Pensions Advisory Service (Opas)
11 Belgrave Road
London SW1V 1RB
Tel: 020 7233 8080
Website: www.opas.org.uk
For general advice on company and individual pensions.

Pension Schemes Registry
PO Box 1NN
Newcastle-upon-Tyne
NE99 1NN
Tel: 0191 225 6316
Website: www.opra.gov.uk
To track down old company pension schemes.

The Occupational Pensions Regulatory Authority (Opra)
Invicta House
Trafalgar Place
Brighton BN1 4DW
Tel: 01273 627600
Website: www.opra.gov.uk
For general complaints about the running of company pension schemes. Opra will not handle individual complaints.

Websites: www.fsa.gov.uk
www.stakeholder.opra.gov.uk
Stakeholder helpline at Opas: 0845 601 2923
Department of Work and Pensions' pensions line: 0845 731 3233
For information on stakeholder pensions.

Useful names, addresses and websites

Specialist annuity advisers

The Annuity Bureau
Enterprise House
59-65 Upper Ground
London SE1 9PQ
Tel: 020 7902 2300
Website: www.annuity-bureau.co.uk

Annuity Direct
32 Scrutton Street
London EC2A 4RQ
Tel: 020 7684 5000
Website: www.annuitydirect.co.uk

Bestinvest
20 Mason's Yard
London SW1Y 6BU
Tel: 020 7321 0100
Website: www.bestinvest.co.uk/pensions

Wentworth Rose
Central House
75-79 Park Street
Camberley
Surrey GU15 3PE
Tel: 0127 626111
Website: www.retirement-advice.co.uk

Home income plans

Safe Home Income Plans (Ship)
c/o Hinton & Wild
1st floor
Parker Court
Knapp Lane
Cheltenham
Gloucs GL50 3QJ
Tel: 01242 539494
Website: www.ship-ltd.co.uk

Where to find a financial adviser

IFA Promotion
17-19 Emery Road
Brislington
Bristol BS4 5PF
Tel: 0800 085 3250
Website: www.ifap.org.uk

The Money Management Register of Fee-Based Advisers
Freepost 22
SW1 565
London W1E 1BR
Tel: 0870 013 1925
Website: www.ukifadirectory.co.uk

Association of Private Client Investment Managers and Stockbrokers (APCIMS)
112 Middlesex Street
London E1 7HY
Tel: 020 7247 7080
Website: www.apcims.co.uk

Society of Financial Advisers (Sofa)
20 Aldermanbury
London EC2V 7HY
Tel: 020 7417 4442
Website: www.sofa.org
All members of Sofa have the advanced financial planning certificate.

Legal matters

The Law Society
113 Chancery Lane
London WC2A 1PL
Tel: 020 7242 1222
Websites: www.lawsociety.org.uk
www.make-a-will.org.uk

Useful names, addresses and websites

The Law Society of Northern Ireland
Law Society House
98 Victoria Street
Belfast BT1 3JZ
Tel: 02890 231614

The Law Society of Scotland
26 Drumsheugh Gardens
Edinburgh EH3 7YR
Tel: 0131 226 7411
Dial-a-Law information line: 0870 545 5554
Website: www.lawscot.org.uk

Specialist magazines

Money Management
Maple House
149 Tottenham Court Road
London W1P 9LL
Tel: 020 7896 2525
Subscriptions: 020 8606 7545

Planned Savings
69-77 Paul Street
London EC2A 4LQ
Tel: 020 7553 1000
Subscriptions: 01206 772223
These magazines are aimed at professional advisers, with performance statistics and articles on aspects of financial planning.

Moneyfacts
66-70 Thorpe Road
Norwich
Norfolk NR1 1BJ
Tel: 01603 476476
Subscriptions: 01603 476100
Website: www.moneyfacts.co.uk
Publishes a monthly round-up of savings accounts rates. The website contains details of best buys on savings accounts.

Useful names, addresses and websites

Trade bodies

Association of Investment Trust Companies
Durrant House
8-13 Chiswell Street
London EC1Y 4YY
Tel: 0800 085 8520
Websites: www.itsonline.co.uk
www.aitc.co.uk
Provides information on investing in investment trust companies.

Association of Unit Trusts and Investment Funds
65 Kingsway
London WC2B 6TD
Tel: 020 8207 1361
Website: www.investmentfunds.org.uk
Provides information on investing in unit trusts and Oeics.

Proshare
Centurion House
24 Monument Street
London EC3R 8AQ
Tel: 020 7394 5200
Website: www.proshare.org.uk
Advises on setting up investment clubs.

Association of British Insurers
51 Gresham Street
London EC2V 7HQ
Tel: 020 7600 3333
Website: www.abi.org.uk
Publishes information sheets on all aspects of insurance.

Building Societies Association
3 Savile Row
London W1X 1AF
Tel: 020 7437 0655
Website: www.bsa.org.uk

Useful names, addresses and websites

Council of Mortgage Lenders
3 Savile Row
London W1X 1AF
Tel: 020 7440 2255
Website: www.cml.org.uk

Association of Policy Market Makers
Holywell Centre
1 Phipp Street
London EC2A 4PS
Tel: 020 7739 3949
Trade body for dealers in second-hand endowment policies – has a directory of members.

Charities

Age Concern England
Astral House
1268 London Road
London SW16 4ER
Tel: 020 8765 7200
Information line: 0800 009966
Website: www.ageconcern.org.uk

Age Concern Cymru
4th floor
1 Cathedral Road
Cardiff CF1 9SD
Tel: 0292 037 1566

Age Concern Scotland
113 Rose Street
Edinburgh EH2 3DT
Tel: 0131 220 3345

Age Concern Northern Ireland
3 Lower Crescent
Belfast BT7 1NR
Tel: 0289 024 5729

Help the Aged
St James's Walk
Clerkenwell Green
London EC1R 0BE
Tel: 0808 800 6565
Website: www.helptheaged.org.uk
Age Concern and Help The Aged can provide advice and information on many financial matters for retired people.

Another useful website: www.find.co.uk
This will direct you to all other main financial sites.

Courses on pre-retirement planning

A number of colleges and adult education centres run courses on pre-retirement planning and preparation. There are also a number of commercial operations in this field and many large companies provide places on such courses for their employees (and, often, their partners). Such courses can last for an evening or a few days and they will cover many aspects of retirement, not just financial matters.

The Pre-Retirement Association, a registered charity, exists to raise standards in the education and training of pre-retirement advisers. It also runs regular pre-retirement courses which are open to individuals and to companies with employees approaching retirement. The cost for 2001 was £263 plus Vat for one person, £418 plus Vat for a couple, for a two-day, non-residential course.

Pre-Retirement Association
9 Chesham Road
Guildford
Surrey GU1 3LS
Tel: 01483 301170
Website: www.pra.uk.com

Index

Activities of daily living (ADL) 82
Additional voluntary contributions
  (AVC) 44-6, 48-9, 50-51
    added year schemes 44-5
    freestanding 45
    limits on 45-7
    money purchase schemes 31, 45
ADL see Activities of daily living
Age allowance trap 103, 168-9
Annual yield, corporate bond 113
Annuities 61-74, 149-51
    and inheritance tax planning
      150-51
    escalating 64-5
    fixed interest 64-5
    guaranteed period 66
    guaranteed rates 66-7
    how they work 61-2
    impaired life 67
    income frequency 66
    index-linked 64-5
    joint 66
    level 64-5
    open market option 64
    single life 66
    the pensions choice 73-4
    unit-linked 68-9
    when to buy 62-3
    with-profits 68-9
Annuity advisers 179
Annuity rates 67-8
    and money purchase schemes 31-2
Association of Investment Trust
  Companies 128
AVC see Additional voluntary
  contributions
Basic state pension 14-15
    for people over 80 18
    how to claim 15
    qualifying years 16-17
Bonds
    corporate 112-14
    guaranteed equity 108-9
    guaranteed income 107
    life assurance 128-30

  stock-market linked high income 117
  with-profits 115-17
Capital gains tax (CGT) 12, 128, 171-3,
  174-5
Cash 98-100
Cash Isas 105, 106
CGT see Capital gains tax
Charities 183-4
Company pensions 25-42
  and length of service 40-41
  earnings cap 39
  employee's contribution 39
  employer's contribution 39
  extra saving for 43-52
  final salary scheme 26-30. See also
    Final salary scheme
  from former employers 36-7
  maximum benefits 40-41
  maximum cash sums 41
  money purchase schemes 30-36
    See also Money purchase schemes
  problems with 37-8
  tax rules 39-41
  tax-free cash 34-6
  tracing pensions from former
    employers 37
Contracted out from Serps 19
Corporate bonds 112-14
  capital risk 113-14
  charges 113
  credit rating 113
  yield 113
Credit cards 9
Current accounts 8-9
Deeds of variation 160
Deferring state pension 20-21
Early retirement
  and company pension money
    purchase schemes 33-4
  and final salary schemes 28-30
Employers, tracing pensions from 37
Endowment mortgages 11
Endowment policies 80-81
Equities 98-100
Equity-release mortgages 153-4

Index

Escalating annuities 64-5
Executors 159
Final salary scheme 26-30
    commutation factor 28
    from former employers 36-7
    how much will it be 26-7
    taking early retirement 28-30
    taking tax-free cash 27-8, 34-6, 41
Financial advisers 88-92
    complaints about 92-3
    payment for 90-91
    where to find 180
Financial Ombudsman Service 92-3
Financial Services Authority (FSA) 177
Financial Services Compensation Scheme 109
Fixed-interest annuities 64-5
Fixed-interest securities 98-100
Fixed-rate investments 106-8
Free-standing AVCs 45
FSA see Financial Services Authority
Gifts, lifetime 162-4
Gifts, with reservations 164
Gilts 107-8, 111-12
Gilts, index-linked 108
Graduated retirement benefit 19
Guaranteed annuity rates 66-7
Guaranteed equity bonds 108-9
Guaranteed income bonds 107
Guaranteed period, annuities 66
Higher-risk investments 110-130
Home income plans 179
Home responsibilities protection (HRP) 17
Home reversion scheme 152-4
IDR see Internal disputes resolution procedure
IHT see Inheritance tax
Impaired life annuities 67
Income drawdown plans 72-3
Income tax 168-70, 173
    and state pension 22
Income, using your home 152-4
Index-linked annuities 64-5
Index-linked gilts 108
Individual pensions 53-60
Individual savings accounts (Isas) 112, 113, 121-2
    cash 104-5, 106
    maxi 105
    mini 104-5, 106

Inflation, and investment 95-6
Inheritance tax (IHT) 161-2
    and gifts 162-4
    and life assurance 164-5
    and trusts 165-6
    and your home 165
    planning 161-6
    planning, and annuities 150-51
Insurance 9-10, 75-86
    long-term care 81-4
    private medical 84-6
Internal disputes resolution procedure (IDR) 38
Internet banking 8-9
Intestacy
    in England and Wales 156-7
    in Northern Ireland 158
    in Scotland 158
Investing, finding advice 87-94
Investment planning 95-100
    and inflation 95-6
    practical examples 131-148
Investment portfolio 12
Investment trusts 120, 126-8
    tax on, 128
Investments, and tax 101-3
Investments
    capital secure 108-9
    compensation schemes 109-10
    fixed-rate 106-8
    for income 151-2
    for those over 70 147-154
Investments, higher risk 119-130
    individual savings accounts 121-2
    investment trusts 126-8
    life assurance bonds 128-30
    Oeics 122-6
    unit trusts 122-6
Investments, low-risk 101-10
    age allowance trap 103
    and tax position 101-2
    fixed-rate investments 106-8
    variable rate investments 103-6
Investments, medium risk 111-18
    corporate bonds 112-14
    gilts 111-12
    Pibs 114-15
    stock-market linked bonds 117
    with-profits bonds 115-17
Investments, variable rate 103-6
Isas see Individual savings accounts

Index

Joint annuity 66
Legal advice 180–81
Level annuities 64–5
Life assurance bonds 128–30
Life expectancy 2–4
Life insurance 75–81
   and taxes 80
   critical illness option 79
   joint life policies 79
   medical examinations 79
   terminal illness option 79
Lifetime gifts, and inheritance tax 162–4
Living costs, changes after retirement 7–8
Long-term care insurance 81–4
   costs of 83
   immediate care plans 83–4
   lump-sum plans 83
Low-risk investments 101–110
Magazines, specialist 181
Making a will 155–61
Market value adjustment factor (MVAF) 116
Maxi Isa 105
Medical insurance, private 84–6
Medium-risk investments 111–18
MIG see Minimum state guarantee
Mini Isa 105
Minimum income guarantee (MIG) 22–3
Money purchase schemes, company pensions 30–36
   how much will it be 31–2
   investment considerations 32–3
   taking early retirement 33–4
   taking tax-free cash 33, 34–6, 41
Money purchase schemes, from former employers 37
Money purchase schemes, individual pension 53–4
Mortgages 10–11
MVAF see Market value adjustment factor
National Insurance Contributions
   and state pension 15, 16–17
   voluntary contributions 17–18
National Savings certificates 106
National Savings income bonds 106
National Savings pensioners' bonds 106
National Savings rates 107

Occupational Pensions Regulatory Authority (Opra) 38
Oeics see Open-ended investment companies
Office for the Pensions Advisory Service (Opas) 38
Ombudsmen 38, 177–8
Opas see Office for the Pensions Advisory Service
Open-ended investment companies (Oeics) 112, 120, 122–5
   tax on 128
Opra see Occupational Pensions Regulatory Authority
Pension credit 22–3
Pension forecast 17
Pension plans
   company charges 56
   staggered vesting 70–72
Pensions advice 178
Pensions, company 25–42
Pensions, extra saving for 43–52
Pensions, individual 53–60
Pensions, personal 54–5
Pensions, state 13–24
Pensions ombudsman 38
Pensions Schemes Registry 37
Peps see Personal equity plans
Permanent interest-bearing shares (Pibs) 114–15
Personal allowances, income tax 168–9
Personal equity plans (Peps) 105, 121
Personal pensions 54–5
Phased retirement 70–72
Pibs see Permanent interest-bearing shares
Pre-retirement courses 184
Pre-retirement timetable 6–7
Private medical insurance 84–6
Qualifying years, basic state pension 16–17
Raps see Retirement annuity plans
Redemption yield, corporate bond 113
'Rent-a-room' tax relief 154
Retirement, investing in 87–93
Retirement age, state 14
Retirement annuity plans (Raps) 55–6
Retirement planning 5–12
Retiring before pension age 18
Self-assessment deadlines 175–6
Self-invested personal pensions (Sipps) 57

Index

Serps see State earnings-related pension scheme
Shares
   how to buy 120
   income from 119-120
   investing in 130
Single life annuity 66
Sipps see Self-invested personal pensions
Staggered vesting 70-72
Stakeholder pension 47-9, 48-9, 50-51, 54, 59
   and deferred state pension 21
Stamp duty 175
State earnings-related pension scheme (Serps) 19-20
State pensions 13-24
   and income tax 22
   minimum income guarantee 22-3
   pension credit 22-3
   postponing receipt date 20-21
State retirement age 14
Stockbrokers 89
Stock-market linked high income bonds 117
Store cards 9
Tax
   age allowance trap 103
   company pension schemes 39-41
   facts and figures for 2001-2 173-6
   investments 101-3
   investment trusts 128
   life insurance 80

Oeics 128
   planning 167-76
   capital gains tax 171-3
   income tax 168-70
   self-assessment deadlines 175-6
   unit trusts 128
Taxable remuneration 39
Tessa 104-5
Timetable for retirement 6-7
Tracing pensions from former employers 37
Trade organisations 182-3
Trusts, investment 126-8
Trusts, unit 122-6
TV licences 23
Unit trusts 120, 122-6
   tax on 128
Unit-linked annuities 68-9
Variable rate investments 103-6
Widows and widowers, and Serps 20-21
Will 155-60
   deeds of variation 160
   executors 159
   intestacy 156-8
   making 158-60
   revising 160
Winter fuel payments 23
With-profits annuities 68-9
With-profits bonds 115-17
Women, rise in retirement age 14
Working after retirement, and state pension 18